Donna Kooler's
Crocheted Afghans

Donna Kooler's
Crocheted Afghans

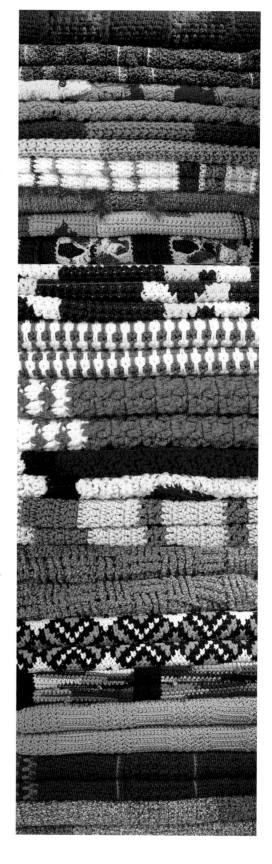

Sterling Publishing Co., Inc. New York
A Sterling/Chapelle Book

Chapelle, Ltd.:

Jo Packham • Sara Toliver • Cindy Stoeckl

Editor: Laura Best
Art Director: Karla Haberstich
Copy Editor: Marilyn Goff
Staff: Kelly Ashkettle, Areta Bingham, Donna Chambers,
  Emily Frandsen, Lana Hall, Susan Jorgensen,
  Jennifer Luman, Melissa Maynard, Barbara Milburn,
  Lecia Monsen, Suzy Skadburg, Kim Taylor,
  Linda Venditti, Desirée Wybrow

If you have any questions or comments, contact:
  Chapelle, Ltd., Inc.,
  P.O. Box 9252, Ogden, UT 84409
  (801) 621-2777 • (801) 621-2788 Fax
  e-mail: chapelle@chapelleltd.com
  web site: chapelleltd.com

Library of Congress Cataloging-in-Publication Data

Kooler, Donna.
  Crocheted afghans / Donna Kooler.
    p. cm.
  "A Sterling/Chapelle Book."
  ISBN 1-4027-0633-2
  1. Afghans (Coverlets) 2. Crocheting--Patterns. I. Title.
TT825 .K693 2004
746.43'0437--dc22

                    2003022669

10 9 8 7 6 5 4 3

Published in paperback in 2005 by Sterling Publishing Co., Inc.
387 Park Avenue South, New York, NY 10016
©2004 by Donna Kooler
Distributed in Canada by Sterling Publishing
c/o Canadian Manda Group, 165 Dufferin Street
Toronto, Ontario, Canada M6K 3H6
Distributed in Great Britain by Chrysalis Books Group PLC
The Chrysalis Building, Bramley Road, London W10 6SP, England
Distributed in Australia by Capricorn Link (Australia) Pty. Ltd.
P.O. Box 704, Windsor, NSW 2756, Australia
Printed and Bound in China
All Rights Reserved

Sterling ISBN 1-4027-0633-2 Hardcover
    ISBN 1-4027-2230-3 Paperback

For information about custom editions, special sales, premium and
corporate purchases, please contact Sterling Special Sales
Department at 800-805-5489 or specialsales@sterlingpub.com.

Creative Director: Donna Kooler
Editor: Marsha Hinkson
Designers: Donna J. Barranti, Amy Brewer,
  Carol Carlile, Joan A. Davis,
  Roberta J. Gardner, C. Yvette Holmes,
  Carol Lykins, Ruthie Marks,
  Marty Miller, Delma Myers,
  Willena Nanton, Nancy Nehring,
  Joy M. Prescott, Janet L. Rehfeldt,
  Kathleen Stuart, Margret Willson,
  Joyce Renee Wyatt

Dedication

It has been my pleasure to have the opportunity of working with members of the Crochet Guild of America. The diversity of this talented group helped to produce the stunning crocheted afghans in this book. I wish to thank the designers: Donna J. Barranti, Amy Brewer, Carol Carlile, Joan A. Davis, Roberta J. Gardner, C. Yvette Holmes, Carol Lykins, Ruthie Marks, Marty Miller, Delma Myers, Willena Nanton, Nancy Nehring, Joy M. Prescott, Janet L. Rehfeldt, Kathleen Stuart, Margret Willson, and Joyce Renee Wyatt for their cooperation, professionalism, and above all, their beautiful work.

There are some very special people I would be remiss not thanking since they had such an important part in making this book possible. Gwen Blakey Kinsler for bringing the designers and Kooler Design Studio together, and last but far from the least, Marsha Hinkson for editing, co-coordinating, managing everything and everyone, and all the while making it appear so effortless.

Enjoy,

Donna Kooler

Soft & Gentle 11

Country Charm 35

Bright & Festive 49

Soft & Gentle

11

Mosaic Ripple Afghan

DESIGNED BY KATHLEEN STUART

Finished size: 30" square

This beautiful reversible afghan looks as if there is a ripple inside a ripple.

MATERIALS:

Yarn: baby sport
Color A—Blue (6 oz.)
Color B—Pink (6 oz.)
Color C—White (8 oz.)
Color D—Yellow (6 oz.)
Crochet hook: size G

SPECIFICS:

Gauges: 18½ rows=4";
point to point 2½"

Basic stitch used: ch, sc

Special stitches used:

Single crochet decrease (sc-dec): (Worked over 3 sts.) Insert hk in st indicated, yo and pl up lp, sk next st, insert hk in next st, yo and pl up lp, yo and pl thr 3 lps on hk.

Long double crochet (Ldc): Yo, insert hk from front to bk in st indicated, yo and pl up long lp, [yo and pl thr 2 lps] twice.

Edge long double crochet decrease (edge Ldc-dec): (Worked over 2 sts.) Yo, insert hk from front to bk in st indicated, yo and pl up long lp, yo and pl thr 2 lps, yo, insert hk from front to bk in next st from first indicated, yo, and pl up long lp, yo and pl thr 2 lps, yo and pl thr 4 lps on hk.

Long double crochet decrease (Ldc-dec): (Worked over 3 sts.) Yo, insert hk from front to bk in st indicated, yo and pl up long lp, yo and pl thr 2 lps, sk next st on working row, yo, insert hk from front to bk in 4th st from first indicated, yo, and pl up long lp, yo and pl thr 2 lps, yo and pl thr 4 lps on hk.

Single crochet long double crochet decrease (sc Ldc-dec): (Worked over 2 sts.) Insert hk in st indicated, yo and pl up lp, yo, insert hk from front to bk in st indicated, yo, and pl up long lp, yo and pl thr 2 lps, yo and pl thr 3 lps on hk.

Color sequence:

Pattern stitch: 2 rows Color A, 2 rows Color C, 2 rows Color A, 2 rows Color C, 2 rows Color B, 2 rows Color C, 2 rows Color B, 2 rows Color C, 2 rows Color D, 2 rows Color C, 2 rows Color D, 2 rows Color C

INSTRUCTIONS:

Row 1: With Color C, ch 146, sc-dec in 2nd ch from hk and next st, *sc in next 4 sts, 3 sc in next st, sc in next 4 sts**, sc-dec in next 3 sts, rep from *across, end last rep at **, sc last 2 sts tog.

12

Row 2 and all even rows: Ch 1, turn, sc in each st across. Chg yarn to next color in sequence.

Row 3: Ch 1, turn, edge Ldc-dec beg in 2nd foundation ch, *sc in next 2 sts, Ldc in 3rd foundation ch from prev Ldc, Ldc in next foundation ch, sk next 2 sts on working row, 3 sc in next st, Ldc in same foundation ch as last prev Ldc, Ldc in next foundation ch, sk next 2 sts on working row, sc in next 2 sts**, Ldc-dec beg in 3rd foundation ch from prev Ldc, rep from *across, end last rep at **, edge Ldc-dec beg in 3rd foundation ch from prev Ldc.

Row 5: Ch 1, turn, sc Ldc-dec beg in first st and in 3rd sc 3 rows below, sk next st on working row, *sc in next 2 sts, Ldc in 3rd st from prev Ldc, sk next st on working row, 3 sc in next st, Ldc in same st as last prev Ldc, sk next st on working row, sc in next 2 sts, Ldc in 3rd st from prev Ldc**, Ldc-dec beg in st next from prev Ldc, Ldc in next st from prev Ldc, sk next 5 sts on working row, rep from *across, end last rep at **, sc Ldc-dec beg in 3rd st from prev Ldc and last sc on working row.

Row 7: Ch 1, turn, sc first 2 sts tog, Ldc in 4th sc 3 rows below, *Ldc in st next to prev Ldc, sk next 2 sts on working row, sc in next 2 sts, 3 Ldc in 3rd st from last prev Ldc, sk next st on working row, sc in next 2 sts, Ldc in 3rd st from prev Ldc, Ldc in st next to prev Ldc, sk next 2 sts on working row**, sc-dec beg in next

st, Ldc in 4th st from prev Ldc, rep from *across, end last rep at **, sc last 2 sts tog.

Row 9: Ch 1, turn, sc first 2 sts tog, sc in next st, Ldc in 5th sc 3 rows below, *Ldc in st next to prev Ldc, sk next 2 sts on working row, sc in next st, 3 sc in next st, sc in next st, Ldc in 2nd st from prev Ldc, Ldc in st next to prev Ldc, sk next 2 sts on working row, sc in next st**, sc-dec beg in next st, sc in next st, Ldc in 8th st from prev Ldc, rep from *across, end last rep at **, sc last 2 sts tog.

Row 11: Ch 1, turn, edge Ldc-dec beg in 2nd st 3 rows below, *sc in next 2 sts, Ldc in 3rd st from prev Ldc, l dc in next st from prev st, sk next 2 sts on working row, 3 sc in next st, Ldc in same st as last prev Ldc, Ldc in next st from prev st, sk next 2 sts on working row, sc in next 2 sts**, Ldc-dec beg in 3rd st from prev Ldc, rep from *across, end last rep at **, edge Ldc-dec beg in 3rd st from prev Ldc.

Rows 12–153: Rep Rows 4–11, eighteen times, end with Row 9.

13

Baby Blocks Afghan

DESIGNED BY MARTY MILLER

Finished size: 36" square

This afghan consists of five different colored panels crocheted together. The final edging is crocheted around the entire afghan.

MATERIALS:

Yarn: 100% cotton
  Color A—White (12 oz.)
  Color B—Green (8 oz.)
  Color C—Yellow (4 oz.)
  Color D—Pink (4 oz.)
  Color E—Baby Blue (4 oz.)
Crochet hook: size H

SPECIFICS:

Gauge: 18 dc=5"

Basic stitches used: sc, hdc, dc

Special stitch used:

Front post double crochet (FPdc): Start dc around post of st in row below, going from front to bk and around to front again. Finish dc as usual. Ch 2 at beg of row counts as FPdc. Hdc at end of row counts as FPdc.

INSTRUCTIONS:

First panel: With Color B, ch 20.
Row 1: (RS) Dc in 4th ch from hk and in each ch across. Ch 2, turn, [18 dc, including the first ch 3].

Row 2: Sk first dc. Fpdc in next st and around each st across, until last ch 3. Hdc in sp bet last st made and ch 3 of prev row. Ch 2, turn, [18 hdc].
Row 3: Sk first st. Fpdc in next st and around each st across, until last ch 2. Hdc in sp bet last st made and ch 2 of prev row. Ch 2, turn.
Rows 4–12: Rep Row 3. At end of Row 12, chg to Color A.
Rows 13–16: Rep Row 3. At end of Row 16, chg to Color C.
Rows 17–76: Rep Row 3, chg colors as fol:
12 rows Color C, 4 rows Color A,
12 rows Color D, 4 rows Color A,
12 rows Color E, 4 rows Color A,
12 rows Color B. FO.

Second panel: Rep First panel, chg colors as fol:
12 rows Color C, 4 rows Color A,
12 rows Color D, 4 rows Color A,
12 rows Color E, 4 rows Color A,
12 rows Color B, 4 rows Color A,
12 rows Color C. FO.

Third panel: Rep First panel, chg colors as fol:
12 rows Color D, 4 rows Color A,
12 rows Color E, 4 rows Color A,
12 rows Color B, 4 rows Color A,
12 rows Color C, 4 rows Color A,
12 rows Color D. FO.

Fourth panel: Rep First panel, chg colors as fol:
12 rows Color E, 4 rows Color A,
12 rows Color B, 4 rows Color A,
12 rows Color C, 4 rows Color A,
12 rows Color D, 4 rows Color A,
12 rows Color E. FO.

Fifth panel: Rep First panel, using the same color sequence.

First panel edging: With RS facing, join Color A in lower-right corner of panel around end st of row. Ch 3. Working around last st of each row, *2 dc at end of next row, 1 dc at end of next row, rep from *to top corner of panel. FO.

Second panel edging: With RS facing, join Color A in upper-left corner of panel around end st of row. Ch 3. Working around last st of each row, dc in same row, *1 dc at end of next row, 2 dc at end of next row. Rep from *to bottom corner of panel. FO. With RS facing, join Color A in lower-right corner of panel, around end st of row. Ch 3. Working around last st of each row, *2 dc at end of next row, 1 dc at end of next row, rep from *to top corner of panel. FO.

Continued on page 16

Continued from page 14

Third and fourth panels edging: Rep Second panel edging.

Fifth panel edging: With RS facing, join Color A in upper left corner of panel around end st of row. Ch 3. Working around last st of each row, dc in same row, *1 dc at end of next row, 2 dc at end of next row. Rep from *to bottom corner of panel. FO.

Joining strips: With Color A, with RS facing out, start at top of panels, join Second panel to First panel by sc in each dc along edge. Rep for Third panel to Second panel, Forth panel to Third panel, Fifth panel to Fourth panel.

Assembly Diagram

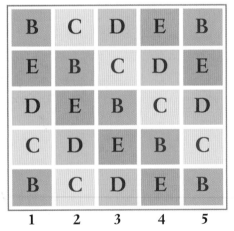

B	C	D	E	B
E	B	C	D	E
D	E	B	C	D
C	D	E	B	C
B	C	D	E	B
1	**2**	**3**	**4**	**5**

Border:

Row 1: With RS facing, join Color A, at upper-right corner in corner sp. Ch 3 (counts as first dc). Dc in same sp. Fpdc in each st across, working one dc in each row of panel edges, and one FPdc around each sc joining edges. At next corner, make 4 dc. Working around last st of each row, *dc in end of next row, 2dc at end of next row. Rep from *to bottom corner. 4 dc in corner. Fpdc in each st across bottom, working one dc in each row of panel edges, and one FPdc around each sc joining edges. 4 dc in corner. Working around last st of each row, *2 dc in end of next row, dc at end of next row. Rep from *to top corner, 2 dc in corner sp. Join with sl st to top of ch 3. Ch 2. Turn.

Row 2: Fpdc in each st around, making 2 FPdc in both of the 2 sts in each corner. Join. Ch 2, turn.

Row 3: Rep Row 2. FO. Weave in ends.

Floating on Air Afghan

DESIGNED BY JANET REHFELDT

Finished size: 30" x 41" with border

The stitch used in this afghan will cause the project to stretch when held up. Keep slip stitches loose but not sloppy, allowing the finished top chain to be the same size as the single crochet stitches in width. Check gauge often to be certain.

MATERIALS:

Yarn: bulky boucle weight
  Multicolored (18 oz.)
Crochet hooks: sizes P, Q

SPECIFICS:

Gauge: 5 sts x 8 rows=4"
Basic stitches used: ch, sc, sl st

INSTRUCTIONS:

Patt=multi of 2.
Row 1: (RS) With Q hk, ch 39, working in bottom lp of ch, sl st in 2nd ch from hk, sc in next ch, *sl st in next ch, sc in next ch *, rep from *to *across, turn [38 sts].
Row 2: Ch 1, sl st in first st, sc in next st *sl st in next st, sc in next st, *rep from *to *across, turn, [38 sts]. Rep Row 2 until piece measures approx 38" from beg. End with a WS row. Turn but do not FO.

Edging: (RS) Using P hk, ch 1, 3 sc in first st (counts as first corner), sc in next 36 sc sts along top edge, work 3 sc in next st (corner made), evenly work 68 sc sts along side edge, work 3 sc in corner, work 36 sc sts along the bottom edge, work 3 sc in last corner, evenly work 68 sc sts along opposite side edge, sl st to first sc. FO. Weave in all ends.

Baby, Baby Afghan

DESIGNED BY RUTHIE MARKS

Finished size: 38" x 52"

This afghan follows an easy sequence. Excepting Rows 1–2 and 103–106, which are v-stitch rows, Rows 3–102 follow a sequence of two v-stitch rows alternating with two 3-double crochet group rows.

MATERIALS:

Yarn: 60% acrylic / 40% nylon
  Color A—White (10½ oz.)
  Color B—Lagoon (3½ oz.)
  Color C—Lilac (3½ oz.)
  Color D—Green Apple (3½ oz.)
  Color E—Mid Blue (3½ oz.)
  Color F—Variegated (7 oz.)
Crochet hooks: sizes E, F

SPECIFICS:

Gauges: 7 V-sts or 3-dc grp=4½";
  5 rows=2½"

Basic stitches used: dc, sc, sl st

Special stitch used:
V-stitch (V-st): Dc, ch, dc.

Color sequence:
By row:
  1–4=A, 5–6=B, 7–8=A,
  9–10=C, 11–12=A, 13–14=D,
  15–16=A, 17–18=E, 19–20=A,
  21–34=Rows 18–5 in reverse,
  35–44=A, 45–52=F, 53–54=A,
  55–62=F, 63–72=A,
  73–102=Rows 34–5 in reverse,
  103–106=A

INSTRUCTIONS:

Row 1: (RS) With Color A, ch 150. Work V-st in 6th ch from hk, *sk 2 ch, V-st in next ch, rep from *across, end sk 2 ch, dc in last ch, turn. (48 V-sts.)

Rows 2–4: Ch 3, V-st in ch-1 sp of each V-st across, end dc in top of tch. Turn.

Row 5: With Color B, ch 3, 3 dc in ch-1 sp of each V-st across, end dc in top of tch. Turn.

Row 6: Ch 3, dc in sp bef first 3-dc grp, *3 dc in sp bef next dc grp, rep from *across, end dc in last sp and dc in top of tch. Turn.

Rows 7–8: With Color A, ch 3, V-st in ch-1 sp of each V-st across, end dc in top of tch. Turn.

Rows 9–104: Fol color sequence chart, rep Rows 5–8 twenty-four times.

Rows 105–106: Rep Rows 7–8.

Edging:

Rnd 1: (RS) With F hk, attach Color A with a sc in any st and sc around, placing 3 sc in each corner st and 2 sc in end of each dc along the sides, sl st to beg sc. FO. Turn.

Rnd 2: With E hk, attach Color F with a sl st in a corner st, ch 3, [dc, ch 2, 2 dc] in corner, *sk 3 sts, [2 dc, ch 2, 2 dc] in next st, rep from *around, adjusting sts if necessary to place [2 dc, ch 2, 2 dc] in each corner st, sl st to beg st. Turn.

Rnd 3: Ch 1, sc in sp bet first 2 dc grps, *6 dc in next ch 2 sp, sc in sp bet next 2 dc grps, rep from *around, placing 7 dc in each corner st, sl st to beg st. FO.

Baby Car Seat Cover

DESIGNED BY NANCY NEHRING

Finished size: 24" x 36"

Each color in this afghan consists of diamonds formed by short rows within the row. Each row is then crocheted to the previous row, creating a patchwork effect.

MATERIALS:

Yarn: homespun
- Color A—Ecru (1 skein)
- Color B—Light Yellow (1 skein)
- Color C—Light Green (1 skein)
- Color D—Lavender (1 skein)

Crochet hook: size L

SPECIFICS:

Gauges: 7 sc=3"; 7 rows=3"; diagonal=4"

Basic stitches used: ch, sl st

INSTRUCTIONS:

Five diamonds:

Foundation row: With Color A, ch 89. In 2nd ch from hk, *[7 sc, sk 1 ch, sl st in next 2 ch, turn, 7 sc, ch 1, turn] three times end with 7 sc, sk 1 ch, sl st in next ch, sk next ch.*Do not turn. First diamond completed. Rep * * four times, end by attaching Color B in last sl st, FO Color A. Turn.

Six diamonds:

Diamond 1: With Color B attached in last sl st, ch 8. In 2nd ch from hk, *7 sc, sl st in next 2 sc of Color A diamond, turn, 7 sc in Color B diamond, ch 1. Turn. *Rep * * three times, end with 7 sc, sl st in last sc of Color A diamond, ch 1. Do not turn.

Diamonds 2–5: Sc in same sp, sc in each end sp of Color A diamond side [6 sc], [sl st in next 2 sc of Color A diamond, turn, 7 sc in Color B diamond, ch 1, turn, 7 sc] three times, end with sl st in last sc of Color A diamond, ch 1. Do not turn. Rep diamond patt three more times.

Diamond 6: Sc in same sp, sc in each end sp of Color A diamond side [6 sc], ch 1, turn, *7 sc in Color B diamond, ch 1, turn. *Rep * * five times, end with 7 sc. FO, turn.

Five diamonds:

Diamond 1: Attach Color C in point of last diamond. Ch 1, sc in same sp, sc in each sp of Color B diamond [6 sc]=7 sc total, *sl st in next 2 sc of Color B diamond, turn, 7 sc in Color C diamond, ch 1, turn, 7 sc*. Rep three times, end with sl st in last sc. First diamond complete. Rep as for First diamond four times, end by attaching Color D in last sl st. FO. Turn.

Rows 4, 8, and 12: Rep Row 2 attaching Color D in last sl st of prev row.

Rows 5, 9, and 13: Rep Row 3 attaching Color A point of last diamond.

Rows 6 and 10: Rep Row 2. Attach Color B in point of last diamond.

Rows 7 and 11: Rep Row 3. Attach Color C in point of last diamond. FO. Weave in all ends. Blk to size.

Zigzag Baby Afghan

DESIGNED BY CAROL CARLILE

Finished size: 44" x 40"

The zigzag popcorn stitches add an interesting relief pattern to complement the lacy delicate border.

MATERIALS:

Yarn: baby sport
Mint Green (32 oz.)
Crochet hook: size G

SPECIFICS:

Gauges: 9 rows=2"; 9 sc=2"

Basic stitch used: sc, sl st

Special stitch used:

Popcorn (pc): 4 dc in st indicated, drop lp from hk, insert hk in first dc of 4-dc grp, pl dropped lp thr.

INSTRUCTIONS:

Ch 151.
Rows 1–5: sc
Row 6: Work 5 sc, ch 4, *20 sc, ch 4, rep from *seven times, end with 5 sc.
Row 7: Rep Row 1.
Row 8: 6 sc, *ch 4, 18 sc, ch 4, 2 sc, ch 4, rep from *six times, end with 6 sc.
Row 9: Rep Row 1.
Row 10: 7 sc, *ch 4, 16 sc, ch 4, 4 sc, rep from *six times, end with 7 sc.
Row 11: Rep Row 1.
Row 12: 8 sc, *ch 4, 14 sc, ch 4, 6

sc, rep from *six times, ch 4, end with 8 sc.
Row 13: Rep Row 1.
Row 14: 9 sc, *ch 4, 12 sc, ch 4, 8 sc, rep from *six times, end with 9 sc.
Row 15: Rep Row 1.
Row 16: 10 sc, *ch 4, 10 sc, rep from *across row.
Row 17: Rep Row 1.
Row 18: 11 sc, *ch 4, 8 sc, ch 4, 12 sc, rep from *six times, end with 11 sc.
Row 19: Rep Row 1.
Row 20: 12 sc, *ch 4, 6 sc, ch 4, 14 sc, rep from *six times, end with 12 sc.
Row 21: Rep Row 1.
Row 22: 13 sc, *ch 4, 4 sc, ch 4, 16 sc, rep from *six times, end with 13 sc.

Row 23: Rep Row 1.
Row 24: 14 sc, *ch 4, 2 sc, ch 4, 18 sc, rep from *six times, end with 14 sc.
Row 25: Rep Row 1.
Row 26: 5 sc, *ch 4, 20 sc, rep from *six times, end with 5 sc.
Rep Rows 6–26 until you have 193 rows. End with 5 rows of sc. (198 rows total.)

Edging:

Row 1: Join yarn to any corner, ch 3 (counts as first dc). Work dc around afghan with 5 dc in each corner. Join with sl st to beg ch 3.
Row 2: *Ch 6, sl st in 3rd ch from hk (picot), ch 3, sk 2 dc of prev row, sc in next dc, rep around blanket, join. FO.

Confetti Baby Afghan

DESIGNED BY JANET REHFELDT

Finished size: 36" x 40" with border

This design is worked entirely in single crochet decreases. The rows of squares resemble squared knotted stitches, while the use of variegated yarn resembles confetti.

MATERIALS:

Yarn: sport weight
  Color A—Variegated (20 oz.)
  Color B—Powder Blue (6 oz.)
Crochet hooks: sizes G, J

SPECIFICS:

Gauge: 18 sts x 16 rows=4"

Basic stitches used: ch, sc, sl st

Special stitches used:

Bobble (B): Work 5 dc sts in same st, drop lp, insert hk into first dc made, pick up dropped lp, pl lp thr first dc.

Picot: [Sl st, ch 2, sl st] in st indicated.

Single crochet decrease (sc-dec): Insert hk into next sc, yo pl up lp, insert hk into ch 1 sp, yo pl up lp, yo pl thr all 3 lps on hk.

Split single crochet (split sc): Insert hk into post of st in prev rnd, yo, pl up a lp, yo, pl thr 2 lps on hk.

INSTRUCTIONS:

Row 1: With Color A and J hk, ch 114, working in bottom lp of ch, sc in 2nd ch from hk, sc in each ch across. Turn. (113 sc.)

Row 2: Ch1, insert hk into first sc, yo, pl up lp, insert hk into next sc, yo, pl up lp, yo pl thr all 3 lps on hk, ch 1, * sc-dec, ch 1*. Rep from *to* to last sc, sc in last sc, Turn.

Row 3: Ch 1, sc-dec over first sc and ch1 sp, ch1, *sc-dec over next sc and ch 1 sp, ch 1 *Rep from *to *across to last st, sc in last st. Rep Row 3 until piece measures 37". FO.

Edging: Using Color B, border worked in chs with split sc and B at corner (multi of 5 + 2).

Foundation: With Color B and G hk, attach yarn at top edge of afghan 2 sts away from corner, sc in same st as join, sc in next st, 3 sc in corner, 147 sc along side edge, 3 sc in corner, 112 sts along bottom edge, 3 sc in corner, 147 sc along opposite side edge, 3 sc in corner, 110 sc along top edge, sl st in first sc to close rnd.

Rnd 1: Split sc in same st as join (2 sts prior to corner), *sk next sc, ch 3, work B in corner, ch 3, sk 1 st, split sc in next st; [ch 4, sk 4 sts, split sc in next st,] to 1 st prior to next corner st,*rep from *to *around.

Rnd 2: Split sc in first split sc of prev rnd, *ch 3, [sc, ch2, sc] in top of B, ch3, split sc in next split sc; [ch 4, split sc in next split sc] to corner B*, rep from *to *around.

Rnd 3: Split sc in first split sc of prev rnd, *ch 2, sc in ch-3 sp, [ch 3, B, ch 3,] in ch 2 sp of corner, sc in ch-3 sp, ch 2, split sc in next split sc; [ch 4, split sc in next split sc] to next corner*, rep from *to *around.

Rnd 4: Split sc in first split sc of prev rnd, *ch 2, split sc in next split sc, ch 3, picot in top of B, ch 3, split sc in next split sc, ch 2, split sc in next split sc; [ch 4, split sc in next split sc] to corner B*, rep from *to *around. FO. Weave in the ends.

Twist and Shout Afghan

DESIGNED BY JOAN A. DAVIS

Finished size: to fit child's car seat 32" wide x 33" high

Row counting is important when working this afghan. Besides the first crossover row, there are ten rows between each crossover row. Crossover rows are worked on odd numbered rows. Gathering rows are worked on even numbered rows. Besides the first loop row, there are seven rows between each gathering row.

MATERIALS:

Yarn: baby weight
　White (21 oz.)
Crochet hooks: sizes F, G
Additional supplies:
　Nonstarch spray
　Paper towels
　Small brass safety pins (50)

SPECIFICS:

Gauges: G hk 10 sts=2";
　11 rows=2"

Basic stitches used: ch, sc, hdc, dc, trc

Special stitches used:

Extended double crochet (exdc):
Yo, insert hk under st or post of dc. Yo, pl thr 1 lp. (See 3 lps on hk.)
Yo pl thr 2 lps. (See 3 lps on hk.) Insert hk into top of next hdc, yo pl thr all 3 lps in motion.

Extended treble crochet (extrc):
Yo twice, insert hk under post of st. Yo, pl thr 1 lp. (See 4 lps on hk.) [Yo, pl thr 2 lps] twice. (See 2 lps left on hk.) Insert hk into top of next hdc, yo pl thr all 3 lps in motion.

Post stitch (post st): Insert hk under post of st, then work yarn around post.

Turning chain (Tch):
FO=with lp on hk, cut thread approx 3"; yo, pl thr lp on hk, twice.

INSTRUCTIONS:

Ch 122, loosely.
Sk 2 chs. In each ch across row: work hdc, ch1. Ch 2. Turn.

Pattern rows:

Row 1: Hdc in next 3 sts (creates selvage edge for patt). Rep the fol twelve times: [Ch 10. Sk 4 ch-1 sps. In next ch 1 sp, work dc. Work dc in next 5 ch-1 sps.] Ch 10. Sk next 4 ch-1 sps. Hdc in last 3 hdc. Ch 2. Turn. Total of 12 sps. *Note:*
- *For ease in counting rows, mark this row with safety pin.*

Row 2: Hdc in next 3 hdc from prev row. Rep the fol eleven times:

[Ch 10. Work hdc in next 6 dc.] Sk next ch-10 sp. Work hdc in next 3 hdc. Ch 2. Turn.

Row 3: Hdc in next 3 hdc. Ch 10. *Note:*
- *You will be working 2 rows below, into patt Row 1.*

Rep the fol eleven times: [exdc in each dc and into hdc on Row 2, complete patt grp, [6 ex dc]. Ch 10. Sk ch 10 sp from prev row.] Sk last ch 10 sp. Work hdc in last 3 hdc. Ch 2. Turn.

Row 4: Hdc in next 3 hdc. Ch 10. Rep the fol eleven times: [Sk next ch 10 sp, work hdc in next 6 exdc. Ch 10.] Work hdc in last 3 hdc. Ch 2. Turn.

Row 5: (Crossover cable row) Hdc in next 3 hdc. Ch 10. Rep the fol eleven times: [Sk next 9 chs. Work sc into 10th ch to help anchor ch-10 to cable. Sk next 3 ex dc on Row 3 and 3 hdc on Row 4, work extrc into the 4th exdc until 2 lps rem on hk. Insert hk into first hdc, yo pl thr all 3 lps in one motion. Work extrc in 5th exdc until 2 lps rem on hk. Insert hk into 2nd hdc. Yo pl thr all 3 lps in one motion. Work extrc in 6th exdc until 2 lps rem on hk. Insert hk into 3nd hdc.

Continued on page 28

Continued from page 26

Yo pl thr all 3 lps in one motion. (First half of crossover completed.) Ch 1. Work extrc in first exdc until 2 lps rem on hk. Insert hk into 4th hdc. Yo pl thr all 3 lps in one motion. Work extrc in 2nd exdc until 2 lps rem on hk. Insert hk into 5th hdc. Yo pl thr all 3 lps in one motion. Work extrc in 3rd ex dc until 2 lps rem on hk. Insert hk into 6th hdc. Yo pl thr all 3 lps in one motion. (Cable crossover completed.) Ch 10.] Hdc in last 3 hdc. Ch 2. Turn.

Row 6: Rep Row 4.

Row 7: (Initial gathering loops row.) Hdc in next 3 hdc. Rep the fol eleven times: [ch 6. Insert hk under first ch 10 lp on patt Row 2. Work exdc as fol around all 6 rows: Exdc=yo, insert hk under lps. Yo, pl thr 1 lp. (See 3 lps on hk.) Yo pl thr 2 lps. (See 3 lps on hk.) Yo pl thr all 3 lps in motion. Ch 6. *Exdc under post of next exdc on Row 5 and first hdc on Row 6. *Rep from *to * five more times. (Total of 6 extended sts worked.)] Ch 6. Work exdc around last grp of lps. Ch 6. Hdc in last 3 hdc. Ch 2. Turn.

Row 8: Rep Row 4.

Row 9: Hdc in next 3 hdc. Ch 10.
Note: First 3 exdc may be behind crossover sts.
Rep the fol twelve times: [Sk next ch 10 sp. *Working under the post of next exdc (2 rows below), work exdc until 2 lps rem on hk. Insert hk into next hdc; yo pl thr, yo, pl thr all 3 lps in one motion. *Rep

bet *s five more times. (Total of 6 exdc.) Ch 10.] Work hdc in last 3 hdc. Ch 2. Turn.

Row 10: Rep Row 4.

Row 11: Rep Row 9.

Row 12: Rep Row 4.

Row 13: Rep Row 9.

Row 14: (Gathering loops row.)
Note:
- *The patt sequence will chg slightly. There will be 7 rows bet each Gathering loops row—always worked on an even numbered row.*

Hdc in next 3 hdc. Rep the fol twelve times: [Ch 6. Exdc around all the ch 10 lps from 7 rows below. Ch 6. Hdc in next 6 hdc.] Hdc in last 3 hdc. Ch 2. Turn.

Row 15: (Crossover cable row.) Hdc in next 3 hdc. Ch 10. Rep the fol eleven times: [Sk next 9 chs. Work sc into 10th ch (this will help anchor the ch-10 to the cable.) Sk next 3 exdc on Row 3 and 3 hdc on Row 4, work extrc into the 4th exdc until 2 lps rem on hk. Insert hk into first hdc, yo pl thr all 3 lps in one motion. Work extrc in 5th exdc until 2 lps rem on hk. Insert hk into 2nd hdc. Yo pl thr all 3 lps in one motion. Work extrc in 6th exdc until 2 lps rem on hk. Insert hk into 3nd hdc. Yo pl thr all 3 lps in one motion. (First half of crossover completed.) Ch 1. Work extrc in first exdc until 2 lps rem on hk. Insert hk into 4th hdc. Yo pl thr all 3 lps in one motion. Work extrc in 2nd exdc until 2 lps rem on hk. Insert hk into 5th hdc. Yo pl thr all 3 lps in one motion. Work extrc

in 3rd exdc until 2 lps rem on hk. Insert hk into 6th hdc. Yo pl thr all 3 lps in one motion. (Cable Crossover completed. There will be 10 rows bet each crossover row and always on an odd-numbered row.) Ch 10.] Hdc in last 3 hdc. Ch 2. Turn.

Rows 16–21: Rep Rows 4 and 9 three times.
Note:
- *First 3 exdc will be behind crossover.*

Row 22: Rep Row 14.

Rows 23–24: Rep Rows 9 and 4.

Row 25: Rep Row 15.

Rows 26-29: Rep Rows 4 and 9 twice.

Row 30: Rep Row 14.

Rows 31–34: Rep Rows 9 and 4 twice.

Row 35: Rep Row 15.

Rows 36–37: Rep Rows 4 and 9.
Note:
- *First 3 exdc will be behind crossover.*

Row 38: Rep Row 14.

Row 39: Rep Row 9.
Note:
- *First 3 exdc will be behind crossover.*

Rows 41–44: Rep Rows 9 and 4 twice.

Row 45: Rep Row 15.

Row 46: Rep Row 14.

Row 47: Rep Row 9.
Note:
- *First 3 exdc will be behind crossover.*

Rows 48–53: Rep Rows 4 and 9 three times.

Row 54: Rep Row 14.

Row 55: Rep Row 15.

Rows 56–61: Rep Rows 4 and 9 three times.

Row 62: Rep Row 14.
Rows 63–64: Rep Rows 9 and 4.
Row 65: Rep Row 15.
Rows 66–69: Rep Rows 4 and 9 twice.
Row 70: Rep Row 14.
Rows 71–74: Rep Rows 9 and 4 twice.
Row 75: Rep Row 15.
Rows 76–77: Rep Rows 4 and 9.
Row 78: Rep Row 14.
Rows 79–84: Rep Rows 9 and 4 three times.
Row 85: Rep Row 15.
Row 86: Rep Row 14.
Row 87: Rep Row 9.
Row 88–93: Rep Rows 4 and 9 three times.
Row 94: Rep Row 14.
Row 95: Rep Row 15.
Rows 96–101: Rep Rows 4 and 9 three times.
Row 102: Rep Row 14.
Rows 103–104: Rep Rows 9 and 4.

Row 105: Rep Row 15.
Rows 106–109: Rep Rows 4 and 9 twice.
Row 110: Rep Row 14.
Rows 111–114: Rep Rows 9 and 4 twice.
Row 115: Rep Row 15.
Rows 116–117: Rep Rows 4 and 9.
Row 118: Rep Row 14.
Rows 119–124: Rep Rows 9 and 4 three times.
Row 125: Rep Row 15.
Row 126: Rep Row 14.
Row 127: Rep Row 9.
Rows 128–133: Rep Rows 4 and 9 three times.
Row 134: Rep Row 14.
Row 135: Rep Row 15.
Rows 136–141: Rep Rows 4 and 9 three times.
Row 142: Rep Row 14.
Row 143: Rep Row 9.
Row 144: Rep Row 4.
Row 145: Rep Row 15.
Rows 146–149: Rep Rows 4 and 9 twice.
Row 150: Rep Row 9.
Row 151: Rep Row 14.
Rows 152–155: Rep Rows 9 and 4 twice.
Row 156: Rep Row 15.
Row 157: Rep Row 4.
Row 158: Rep Row 9.
Row 159: Rep Row 14.
Rows 160–164: Rep Rows 9 and 4 three times.
Row 165: Rep Row 15.
Row 166: Rep Row 14.
Row 167: Rep Row 9.
Rows 168–173: Rep Rows 4 and 9 three times.

Row 174: Rep Row 14.
Row 175: Rep Row 15.
Row 176: Rep Row 4.
Row 177: Rep Row 9.
Rows 178–181: Rep Rows 4 and 9 twice.
Row 182: Rep Row 14.
Row 183: Rep Row 9.
Row 184: Rep Row 4.
Row 185: Rep Row 15.
Rows 186–189: Rep Rows 4 and 9 twice.
Row 190: Rep Row 14.
Rows 191–194: Rep Rows 9 and 4 twice.
Row 195: Rep Row 15.
Row 196: Rep Row 4.
Row 197: Rep Row 9.
Row 198: Rep Row 14.
Row 199: Rep Row 9.
Row 200: Rep Row 4. FO.

Patt Edging:

With RS facing, attach yarn in the middle of row just completed.
Note:
• *You do not want an edge on a corner.* Work the fol row four times: Hdc in each st until you reach the corner. Work corner as fol: 2 hdc, ch3, 2hdc, in corner st. Work hdc along side edge of each row. Cont until around for border. Work border as fol: Sc, ch 4. Work trc in same st as sc just made. Rep fol around afghan: Sk 2 sts. Work sc in next st. Ch 4. Work trc in same st as sc just made.
Note:
• *Because of the cable patt, you may need to blk afghan.*

Pink Square Afghan

DESIGNED BY CAROL CARLILE

Finished size: 46" x 38"

A basic popcorn stitch adds dimension to this simple design afghan, dressed up with a delicate shell border.

MATERIALS:

Yarn: sport weight
    Color A—Pink (26 oz.)
Crochet hook: size G

SPECIFICS:

Gauges: 9 rows=2"; 9 sc=2"

Basic stitch used: sc

Special stitch used:
Simple popcorn (pc)=ch 4.

INSTRUCTIONS:

Ch 141.
Row 1: Work even in sc.
Row 2: 10 sc, *ch 4, 10 sc, rep from *across row end with 10 sc.
Rows 3–8: Rep Rows 1–2 three times.
Row 9: Rep Row 1
Row 10: 2 sc, *ch 4, 2 sc, rep from *across row. This completes one patt set. Rep Rows 1–10 until you have 20 blks in length, end with row 9. (207 total rows.)

Edging:

Row 1: Work 1 row of dc around perimeter, work 5 dc in each corner.
Row 2: Work 1 row of shells around perimeter as fol: Sc in first st, sk 1 st, 5 dc in next st to create shell, sk 1 st, sc in next st, rep around perimeter working 9 dc shells in each corner. FO.

Quick and Easy Afghan

DESIGNED BY MARTY MILLER

Finished size: 36" square

This afghan is a simple pattern where the gauge is not very important to the overall project.

MATERIALS:

Yarn: 98% acrylic/2% polyester
Color A—Variegated (24 oz.)
Crochet hook: size N

SPECIFICS:

Gauge: 5 FPdc=5 rows=3"

Basic stitches used: ch, dc, hdc

Special stitch used:

Front post double crochet (FPdc): Start dc around post of st in row below, going from front to bk and around to front again. Finish dc as usual. Turn ch 2 at beg of row counts as FPdc for next row. Last hdc in each row counts as FPdc.

INSTRUCTIONS:

Ch 62.

Row 1: Dc in 4th ch from hk and in each ch across. Turn. [60 dc, including first ch 3].

Row 2: Ch 2. Sk first st. Fpdc around next dc and each dc across, until last ch 3. Hdc bet last FPdc made and the ch 3 of prev row. Turn. [60 FPdc].

Row 3: Ch 2. Sk first st. Fpdc around next st, and around each st across, until last ch 2. Hdc bet last FPdc made and ch 2 of prev row. Turn. [60 FPdc].

Rows 4–60: Rep Row 3. At end of Row 60. FO. Weave in ends.

Ruffle Baby Afghan

DESIGNED BY C. YVETTE HOLMES

Finished size: 45" square

This afghan is worked with eight sets of v-stitches between two post double crochet stitches (six sets of post stitches.) The afghan is then finished with an extra-wide ruffle.

MATERIALS:

Yarn: sports weight
Color A—Multicolored Pastel or Yellow (5 skeins) (both pictured)
Crochet hook: size I
Additional supplies:
Stitch marker

SPECIFICS:

Gauge: 8 sets of V-sts=6"
Basic stitches used: hdc, dc
Special stitches used:
Back post double crochet (BPdc): Start dc around post of st in row below, going from bk to front and around to bk again. Finish dc as usual.
Front post double crochet (FPdc): Start dc around post of st in row below, going from front to bk and around to front again.

Finish dc as usual.
V-stitch (V-st): Dc, ch, dc.

INSTRUCTIONS:

Ch 101 loosely.
Row 1: Dc in 4th ch from hk; dc in next st, *[sk 1 ch, work V-st in next ch] eight times, sk 1 ch, work 1 dc in each of the next 2 ch st**, rep from *to **across row until 1 ch rem. Dc in last ch. Turn. (Total of 40 V-sts and 6 dc grp.)
Row 2: Ch 3. *Work FPdc around next 2 dc, [work V-st in center of V-st from prev row] eight times. **Rep from *to **across row to last 3 dc. Work FPdc around next 2 dc, dc in top of last dc. Turn.
Row 3: Ch 3. *Work BPdc around next 2 FPdc, [work V-st in center of V-st from prev row] eight times. **Rep from *to **across row to last 3 sts. Work BPdc around next 2 FPdc, dc in top of last dc. Turn.
Row 4: Ch 3. *Work FPdc around next 2 BPdc, [work V-st in center of V-st from prev row] eight times. **Rep from *to **across row to last 3 sts. Work FPdc around next 2 BPdc, dc in top of last dc. Turn. Rep Rows 3–4 until length reaches 35". End with WS row.

Border:
Rnd 1:
Side 1 (Top): Ch 2. Work 1 hdc in each dc across row up to last st on row. Work 3 hdc in last st.
Side 2: Working along side of afghan, work 1 hdc evenly sp until next corner is reached. Work 3 hdc in corner.
Side 3 (Bottom): Working along bottom of afghan, work 2 hdc bet each pair of V-st and work 2 hdc bef and aft each set of post sts until next corner is reached. Work 3 hdc in corner.
Side 4: Working along side of afghan, work 1 hdc evenly sp until next corner is reached. Work 2 hdc in corner. Place a marker in last hdc to identify this corner as starting corner. Place marker in center st of rem three corners.

Border:
Rnd 2:
Work 1 hdc in same corner. Cont around each side working 1 hdc in each hdc until starting st marker is reached. In each corner work 3 hdc in center st (marked with st markers) of prev rnd 3 hdc grp.

Continued on page 34

32

Continued from page 32
Ruffle:

Rnd 1: Ch 5, sc in last hdc bef starting st marker. (This st now contains hdc, ch5, sc.) Working in next st (the center hdc with starting st marker), [ch 5, sc in same hdc] twice. Ch 5, sc in next hdc. +Along the side *[ch 5, sk 1 hdc, work 1 sc in next st] three times. [Ch 5, sc in same st]. **Rep from *to **until next 3 hdc grp is reached. At corner [ch 5, sc in first st in 3 hdc grp]. Working in center hdc, [ch 5, sc in center hdc] twice. Ch 5, sc in 3rd hdc. ++ Rep from + to ++ around for rem sides and corners. Do not join.

Rnd 2: At starting corner, ch 7, sc in first lp in corner grp. Working in center ch lp, [ch 7, sc in same lp] twice. Ch 7, sc in next lp. +Along the side work *[ch 7, 1 sc in next lp] four times. [Ch 7, sc in same lp] **. Rep from *to **until next corner grp is reached. At corner work [ch 7, sc in first lp in corner grp]. Working in center ch lp, [ch 7, sc in center ch lp] twice. Ch 7, sc in next lp. ++ Rep from + to ++ around for rem sides and corners.

Rnd 3: At starting corner, ch 7, sc in first lp in corner grp. Working in center ch lp, [ch 7, sc in center lp] twice. Ch 7, sc in next lp. + Along side, work *[ch 7, 1 sc in next lp] **. Rep from *to **until next corner grp is reached. At corner work [ch 7, sc in first lp in corner grp]. Working in center ch lp, [Ch 7, sc in center lp] twice. Ch 7, sc in next lp. ++ Rep from + to ++ around for rem sides and corners.

Subsequent rnds: Rep Rnd 3 until ruffle is approx 4¾".

Next rnd: Work [ch 7, work 1 sc in next ch lp] around afghan.

Final rnd: *Work 7 hdc in next lp, sl st in top of sc **. Rep around. Join to first hdc. FO. Weave in ends.

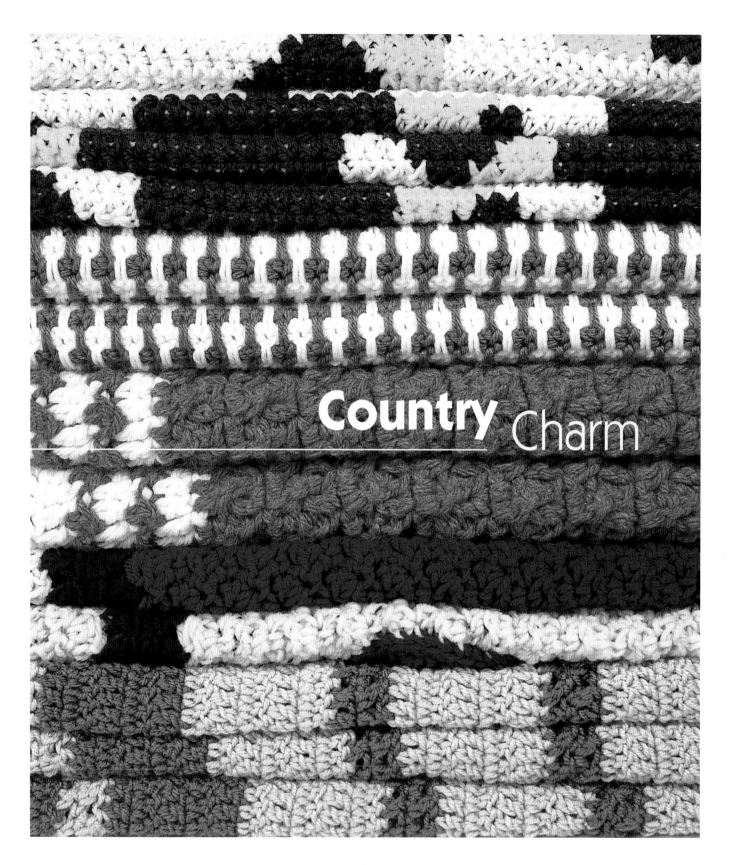

Country Charm

Cozy Country Afghan

DESIGNED BY AMY BREWER

Finished size: 43" x 55"

The body of this afghan is worked with single strands of two colors, two rows at a time, so you can drop the unused color until you need it again. The long single crochet lends itself to the creation of a very thick fabric. The edging is worked with a double strand to match the thickness of the body.

MATERIALS:

Yarn: 100% acrylic, soft worsted weight
   Color A—Country Blue (30 oz.)
   Color B—Off-white (30 oz.)
Crochet hook: size K

SPECIFICS:

Gauges: 3 sc=1";
   7 rows sc=2"

Basic stitches used: ch, sc, sl st

Special stitch used:

Long single crochet (Lsc): Insert hk into designated st, yo, draw up a lp, yo, draw thr both lps on hk. (Basically you are making st longer by sc in row(s) below.)

INSTRUCTIONS:

Multiple of 2. With Color A, ch 116.
Row 1: Sc in 2nd ch form hk [ch 1, sk next ch, sc in next ch] across.
Row 2: Ch 1, turn, sc in first sc, sc in ch 1 sp, [sk next st, 2 sc in next ch 1 sp] rep across, sc in last st, chg to Color B in last st.
Row 3: Ch 1, turn, sc in first st, [ch 1, Lsc in next sk ch on beg ch] across, sc in last st.
Row 4: Ch 1, turn, sc in first st, [sk Lsc, 2 sc in next ch 1 sp] across, one sc in last ch 1 sp, sc in last st, chg to Color A.
Row 5: Ch 1, turn, sc in first st, [ch 1, sk next st, Lsc in sk st 3 rows down] across, ch 1, sc in last st.
Row 6: Ch 1, turn, sc in first st, 1 sc in first ch 1 sp, [sk Lsc, 2 sc in next ch 1 sp] across* sc in last st, chg to Color B.
Row 7: Ch 1, turn. Sc in first st, ch 1, Lsc in sk st 3 rows down, [ch 1, sk next st, Lsc in sk st 3 rows down] across, sc in last st. Rep Rows 4–7 until afghan measures 53", then rep Row 4 once more.
Last row: Ch 1, turn, sc in first 2 sts, [Lsc in next st 3 rows down, sc in next st] rep across, sc in last st. Do not FO.

Edging: Join a 2nd strand of Color A in same sp as last st. Working with double strand do not turn, working down side of afghan.
Rnd 1: Ch 1, 2 sc in end of first row, [sc in end of next row, sk next row] across. Working in free lps of beg ch, 3 sc in first free lp, 1 sc in each lp across, 3 sc in last free lp. Working up other side, sk first row, [sc in end of next row, sk next row] across. Work 3 sc in first st of last row, 1 sc in each st across, sc in same st as first sc, sl st in first sc to join.
Rnds 2–3: Ch 1, sc in first st, work sc evenly across and 3 sc in corners all around. Sl st in first sc to join. FO. Chg to Color B.
Rnd 4: Rep Rnd 2.
Rnd 5: Sl st in each st around. FO.

36

Galaxy Afghan

DESIGNED BY DONNA J. BARRANTI

Finished size: 48" x 59"

The star stitches and color changes make this colorful afghan enjoyable to work.

MATERIALS:

Yarn: sport weight
    A—Hunter Green (30 oz.)
    B—Off-white (20 oz.)
    C—Yellow (10 oz.)
Crochet hooks: size F, G

SPECIFICS:

Gauge:
    9 star sts and 10 rows=4"

Basic stitch used: sc. rsc

Special stitches used:

Beginning star stitch (beg star st): Yo insert hk in 3rd ch from hk, yo and pl up a lp, yo, insert hk in eyelet of next star st, yo and pl up a lp, yo and draw thr all 5 lps on hk, ch 1 to close star st and form eyelet.

Star stitch (star st): Yo, insert hk in same eyelet as last leg of last star st made, yo and pl up a lp, yo, insert hk in eyelet of next star st, yo and pl up a lp, yo and draw thr all 5 lps on hk, ch 1 to close star st and form eyelet.

Ending star stitch (end star st): Yo, insert hk in same eyelet as last leg of last star st made, yo and pl up a lp, yo, insert hk in sp bef turning ch, yo and pl up a lp, yo and draw thr all 5 lps on hk.

Notes:
- *With Color A, ch 227 loosely, place marker in 3rd ch from hk for st placement. (227 ch.)*
- *To chg color at beg of a row, hk new yarn and draw thr lp on hk, forming first ch of beg ch 3. To chg color within a row, work star st to within one step of completion (1 lp on hk), hk new yarn, and draw thr lp on hk, forming ch long eyelet. Work over unused color, holding yarn with normal tension and keeping it to WS of work.*

INSTRUCTIONS:

Row 1: (RS) Yo, insert hk in 3rd ch from hk, yo and pl up a lp, yo, sk next ch, insert hk in next ch, yo and pl up a lp, yo and draw thr all 5 lps on hk, *ch 1 to close star st and form eyelet, yo, insert hk in same ch as last leg of star st just made, yo and pl up a lp, yo, sk next ch, insert hk in next ch, yo and pl up a lp, yo and draw thr all 5 lps on hk; rep from *across. (112 star sts.)

Note:
- *First ch of turning ch on fol row will serve as eyelet for end star st.*

Row 2: Ch 3, turn; work beg star st, work 6 star sts chg to Color B in last st, *work star st chg to Color A, work 8 star sts chg to Color C in last st; work star st chg to Color A in last st, work 12 star sts; chg to Color B in last st, rep from *three times more, work star st chg to Color A, work 8 star sts chg to Color C in last st; work star st chg to Color A in last st, work 6 star sts, work end star st.

Row 3: Ch 3, turn; work beg star st, work 6 star sts chg to Color C in last st, *work 2 star sts chg to Color A, work 6 star sts chg to Color B in last st; work 2 star sts chg to Color A in last st, work 12 star sts; chg to Color C in last st, rep from *three times more, work 2 star sts chg to Color A, work 6 star sts chg to Color B in last st; work 2 star sts chg to Color A in last st, work 6 star sts, work end star st.

Row 4: Ch 3, turn; work beg star st, work 6 star sts chg to Color B in last st, *work 3 star sts chg to Color A, work 4 star sts chg to Color C in last st; work 3 star sts chg to Color A in last st, work 12 star sts; chg to Color B in last st, rep from *three times more, work 3 star sts chg to Color A, work 4 star sts chg to Color C in last st;

Continued on page 44

Continued from page 42

work 3 star sts chg to Color A in last st, work 6 star sts, work end star st.

Row 5: Ch 3, turn; work beg star st, work 6 star sts chg to Color C in last st, *work 4 star sts chg to Color A, work 2 star sts chg to Color B in last st; work 4 star sts chg to Color A in last st, work 12 star sts; chg to Color C in last st, rep from *three times more, work 4 star sts chg to Color A, work 2 star sts chg to Color B in last st; work 4 star sts chg to Color A in last st, work 6 star sts, work end star st.

Row 6: Ch 3, turn; work beg star st, work 6 star sts chg to Color B in last st, *work 5 star sts chg to Color C in last st; work 5 star sts chg to Color A in last st, work 12 star sts; chg to Color B in last st, rep from *three times more, work 5 star sts chg to Color C in last st; work 5 star sts chg to Color A in last st, work 6 star sts, work end star st.

Row 7: Ch 3, turn; work beg star st, work star st chg to Color B in last st, *work 15 star sts chg to Color C in last st, work 5 star sts chg to Color A in last st; work 2 star sts chg to Color B in last st; rep from *three times more, work 15 star sts chg to Color C, work 5 star sts chg to Color A in last st; work star st, work end star st.

Row 8: Ch 3, turn; work beg star st, work 2 star sts chg to Color C in last st, *work 4 star sts chg to

Color B in last st, work 14 star sts chg to Color A in last st; work 4 star sts chg to Color C in last st; rep from *three times more, work 4 star sts chg to Color B, work 14 star sts chg to Color A in last st; work 2 star sts, work end star st.

Row 9: Ch 3, turn; work beg star st, work 3 star sts chg to Color B in last st, *work 13 star sts chg to Color C in last st, work 3 star sts chg to Color A in last st; work 6 star sts chg to Color B in last st; rep from *three times more, work 13 star sts chg to Color C, work 3 star sts chg to Color A in last st; work 3 star sts, work end star st.

Row 10: Ch 3, turn; work beg star st, work 4 star sts chg to Color C in last st, *work 2 star sts chg to Color B in last st, work 12 star sts chg to Color A in last st; work 8 star sts chg to Color C in last st; rep from *three times more, work 2 star sts chg to Color B, work 12 star sts chg to Color A in last st; work 4 star sts, work end star st.

Row 11: Ch 3, turn; work beg star st, work 5 star sts chg to Color B in last st, *work 11 star st chg to Color C, work star sts chg to Color A in last st; work 10 star sts chg to Color B in last st; rep from *three times more, work 11 star st chg to Color C, work star sts chg to Color A in last st; work 5 star sts, work end star st.

Row 12: Ch 3, turn; work beg star st, work 5 star sts chg to Color B in last st, *work 11 star sts chg to Color C, work star st chg to Color

A in last st; work 10 star sts chg to Color B in last st; rep from *three times more, work 11 star sts chg to Color C, work star st chg to Color A in last st; work 5 star sts, work end star st.

Row 13: Ch 3, turn; work beg star st, work 4 star sts chg to Color B in last st, *work 12 star sts chg to Color C, work 2 star sts chg to Color A in last st; work 8 star sts chg to Color B in last st; rep from *three times more, work 12 star sts chg to Color C, work 2 star sts chg to Color A in last st; work 4 star sts, work end star st.

Row 14: Ch 3, turn; work beg star st, work 3 star sts chg to Color B in last st, *work 13 star sts chg to Color C, work 3 star sts chg to Color A in last st; work 6 star sts chg to Color B in last st; rep from *three times more, work 13 star sts chg to Color C, work 3 star sts chg to Color A in last st; work 3 star sts, work end star st.

Row 15: Ch 3, turn; work beg star st, work 2 star sts chg to Color C in last st, *work 4 star sts chg to Color B, work 14 star sts chg to Color A in last st; work 4 star sts chg to Color C in last st; rep from *three times more, work 4 star sts chg to Color B, work 14 star sts chg to Color A in last st; work 2 star sts, work end star st.

Row 16: Ch 3, turn; work beg star st, work star st chg to Color B in last st, *work 15 star sts chg to Color C, work 5 star sts chg to Color A in last st; work 2 star sts chg to Color B in last st; rep from *three times more, work 15 star sts chg to Color C, work 5 star sts chg to Color A in last st; work star st, work end star st.

Row 17: Ch 3, turn; work beg star st, work 6 star sts chg to Color B in last st, *work 5 star sts chg to Color C in last st; work 5 star sts chg to Color A in last st, work 12 star sts; chg to Color B in last st, rep from *three times more, work 5 star sts chg to Color C in last st; work 5 star sts chg to Color A in last st, work 6 star sts, work end star st.

Row 18: Ch 3, turn; work beg star st, work 6 star sts chg to Color C in last st, *work 4 star sts chg to Color A, work 2 star sts chg to Color B in last st; work 4 star sts chg to Color A in last st, work 12 star sts; chg to Color C in last st, rep from *three times more, work 4 star sts chg to Color A, work 2 star sts chg to Color B in last st; work 4 star sts chg to Color A in last st, work 6 star sts, work end star st.

Row 19: Ch 3, turn; work beg star st, work 6 star sts chg to Color B in last st, *work 3 star sts chg to Color A, work 4 star sts chg to Color C in last st; work 3 star sts chg to Color A in last st, work 12 star sts; chg to Color B in last st, rep from *three times more, work 3 star sts chg to Color A, work 4 star sts chg to Color C in last st; work 3 star sts chg to Color A in last st, work 6 star sts, work end star st.

Row 20: Ch 3, turn; work beg star st, work 6 star sts chg to Color C in last st, *work 2 star sts chg to Color A, work 6 star sts chg to Color B in last st; work 2 star sts chg to Color A in last st, work 12 star sts; chg to Color C in last st, rep from *three times more, work 2 star sts chg to Color A, work 6 star sts chg to Color B in last st; work 2 star sts chg to Color A in last st, work 6 star sts, work end star st.

Row 21: Ch 3, turn; work beg star st, work 6 star sts chg to Color B in last st, *work star st chg to Color A, work 8 star sts chg to Color C in last st; work star st chg to Color A in last st, work 12 star sts; chg to Color B in last st, rep from *three times more, work star st chg to Color A, work 8 star sts chg to Color C in last st; work star st chg

to Color A in last st, work 6 star sts, work end star st.

Rows 22–23: Ch 3, turn; with Color A only, work beg star st, work 110 star sts, work end star st.

Rows 24–134: Rep Rows 2–23.

Edging:

Rnd 1: Ch 3, do not turn; work beg star st, work 133 star sts evenly spaced across ends ofropws (working in eyes and ch 3 spaces); ch 3 work beg star st, work 111 star sts, ch 3 work beg star st, work 133 star sts evenly spaced across end of rows (working in eyes and ch 3 spaces.)

Rnd 2: Using G hk, attach second strand of Color A, do not turn (work from left to right), with two strands of Color A, work rsc around; join with a sl st. FO.

Here's My Heart Afghan

DESIGNED BY JOY M. PRESCOTT

Finished size: 54" x 72"

The various squares are made separately, then crocheted together. The hearts are individually crocheted, then sewn onto the afghan.

MATERIALS:

Yarn: 4-ply worsted weight:
Color A—Off-white (14 oz.)
Color B—Black (10 oz.)
Color C—Burgundy (12 oz.)
Color D—Grey Heather (12 oz.)
Color E—Warm Brown (8 oz.)
Crochet hooks: sizes G, K, N
Additional supplies:
Tapestry needle

SPECIFICS:

Gauges: 4 sts=2";
4 rows=2" in patt st

Basic stitches used: ch, dc, sc, sl st

Special stitch used:
V-stitch (V-st): Dc, ch, dc.

Color sequence:
Pattern stitch:
Row 1: Ch amount specified for square or rectangle, sc in 4th ch from hk (counts as 2 sts), *dc in next st, sc in next st, rep from *across.
Row 2: Ch 3 (counts as first dc),

*sc in next dc, dc in next sc, rep from *across, end with sc in top of starting ch. Rep Row 2 for specified number of rows.

INSTRUCTIONS:

Small rectangle: (Make three Color D, two Color A, three Color C, two Color E.) Ch 18 and work in patt st for 22 rows.
Square: (Make four Color D, three Color A, three Color C, two Color E.) Ch 24 and work in patt st for 22 rows.
Large rectangle: (Make one Color A, one Color C, two Color E.) Ch 18 and work in patt st for 44 rows.

Large heart: (Make three.)
Row 1: With K hk and Color C, ch 2, 2 sc in 2nd ch from hk, ch 1. Turn each row unless specified otherwise.
Row 2: 2 sc in each sc. (4 sts.)
Row 3: 2 sc in first sc, sc across to last sc, 2 sc in last sc. (6 sts.)
Row 4: Sc in each st across.
Rows 5–8: Rep Rows 3–4. (8, 10 sts.)
Rows 9–10: Rep Row 3. (12, 14 sts.)
Row 11: Rep Row 4. (14 sts.)
Upper-right Row 12: Sc in 5 st, dec in 2 sts. Turn. (6 sts.)
Row 13: Dec in first 2 st, sc in 2 sts, dec in next 2 sts. (4 sts.)

Row 14: Dec twice. (2 sts.) FO.
Upper-left Row 12: Join with sl st in next unworked st on Row 11. Ch 1, dec in this and next st, sc in 5 sts. (6 sts.)
Row 13: Rep Row 13 of Upper-right.
Row 14: Rep Row 14 of Upper-right. Do not FO.

Finishing: Ch 1, sc around heart, working 2 sc in bottom point and outside corners of Upper-right and Upper-left, dec in center top bet Upper-right and Upper-left.

Skinny heart: (Make five.)
Row 1: With Color C and K hk, ch 2, 1 sc in 2nd ch, ch 1. Turn each row unless specified otherwise.
Row 2: 2 sc in sc. (2 sts.)
Row 3: 2 sc in each sc, sc in sc. (3 sts.)
Row 4: Sc in 2 sc, 2 sc in next sc. (4 sts.)
Rows 5–7: Sc in each sc across.
Row 8: Sc in each sc to last sc, 2 sc in last sc. (5 sts.)
Upper-right Row 9: 2 sc in sc, sc in next sc, sl st in next st, ch 1. Turn. (3 sts.)
Row 10: Sk sl st, sl st in sc, 2 sc in next sc, sc in sc. (3 sts.)
Row 11: Sc in next 2 sc, sl st in next st. (2 sts.)

Continued on page 48

Continued from page 46

Row 12: Sk sl st, sl st in sc, 2 sc in next st, sl st in next st. FO.

Upper-left Row 9: Join with sl st in same st as last st worked on Row 9, ch 1, sc in next sc, 2 sc in next st.

Row 10: Sc in 2 sc, sl st in next st.

Row 11: Sk sl st, sl st in 2 sc. Finish same as for Large heart.

Finishing:

For each square and rectangle:

With Color B and K hk, join with sl st in any corner, ch 4, V-st in same st as joining, cont to work

V-st around edge with [dc, ch, V-st] in ea corner as fol:

Squares: 10 V-sts along each edge.

Small rectangles: 7 V-sts along top, 10 along sides.

Large rectangles: 7 V-sts along top, 22 along sides. In each corner, work [dc, ch, V-st]. Sew squares and rectangles tog using Assembly Diagram for placement.

Sew hearts to squares, working only in top side of afghan so sts do not show thr on bk.

Border:

Row 1: With Color B and K hk, join with sl st in any st along edge of afghan, ch, sc in same st and in each st around. FO.

Row 2: With Color C and G hk, join with sl st in any st, ch, [dc in next st, sl st in next st] around afghan, join with sl st in first st. FO.

Assembly Diagram

Key:
grey heather
off-white
warm brown
burgundy

48

Bright & Festive

Emerald Isle Afghan

DESIGNED BY RUTHIE MARKS

Finished size: 44" x 59"

This afghan combines bright color and popcorn stitch relief to create its own character and style.

MATERIALS:

Yarn: worsted weight
Color A—Variegated (30 oz.)
Color B—Contrasting (7 oz.)
Crochet hook: size J
Additional supplies:
Tapestry needle

SPECIFICS:

Gauge: 6 sc and 3 dc rows=2"

Basic stitches used: bk lp, dc, sl st

Special stitch used:

4-double crochet popcorn (4-dc pc): Work 4 dc into one st. Take hk out of working lp and insert into top of the first dc made, from front to bk. Pick up working lp and draw thr to close pc.

Note:
• *To maintain continuity, count sts aft each Row 19.*

INSTRUCTIONS:

Row 1: (WS) With Color A, ch 137. Dc in 4th ch from hk and in each ch across. Turn. (135 dc.)

Row 2: Ch 3 (counts as first dc), sk first st, dc in ft lp only of next st, *dc in bk lp only of next st, dc in ft lp only of next st, rep from last st, dc in tch. Turn.

Rows 3–9: Rep Row 2, at end of Row 9 FO. Turn.

Row 10: (RS) Attach Color B with sl st, ch 1 and loosely sl st in both lps of each st across. FO. Turn.

Row 11: With Color A, sc thr top lp only of each sl st across. Turn.

Rows 12–13: Ch 1, sc in each st across. Turn.

Row 14: Ch 1, sc in first 12 sts, 4-dc pc in next st, *sc in next 10 sts, 4-dc pc, rep from *to last 12 sts, sc in last 12 sts. Turn.

Rows 15–17: Ch 1, sc thr both lps of each st across. FO. Turn.

Row 18: Attach Color B with a sl st, ch 1 and loosely sl st in both lps of each st across. FO. Turn.

Row 19: With Color A ch 3, sk first st, dc thr top lp only of each sl st across. Turn. (135 dc.)

Rows 20–109: Rep Rows 2–19 five times.

Rows 110–117: Rep Row 2. Do not FO. Turn.

Edging:

Rnd 1: (RS) Ch 1, sc in each st around, placing 3 sc in each corner st, sl st to beg st. Turn.

Rnd 2: Ch 1, sc in each st around, placing 3 sc in each corner st, sl st to beg st. FO. Turn.

Rnd 3: With Color B, attach yarn with a sl st, ch 1 and loosely sl st thr both lps of each st around, placing [sl st, ch 1, sl st] in each corner st. FO. Turn.

Rnd 4: Attach A with a sc in any st, sc thr top lp only of each sl st around, sl st to first sc. FO. Turn.

Rnd 5: Attach Color B with a sl st in any st, ch 1, and [sl st, ch] in each st around, sl st to beg sl st, FO.

Fiesta Time Afghan

DESIGNED BY RUTHIE MARKS

Finished size: 46" x 60"

This bright afghan is a mirrored pattern of multi-colored lines and bobbles.

MATERIALS:

Yarn: worsted weight
Color A—Off-white (35 oz.)
Color B—Red (9 oz.)
Color C—Green (6 oz.)
Color D—Yellow (6 oz.)
Color E—Blue (6 oz.)
Color F—Coral (6 oz.)
Crochet hook: size I

SPECIFICS:

Gauges: 6 sc or dc=2";
4 rows (dc, sc, dc, sc)=2"

Basic stitches used: dc, sc, sl st

Special stitches used:

3-double crochet bobble
(3-dcB): Yo, insert hk into st, pl yarn thr, yo and pl thr 2 lps (2 lps on hk), yo, insert hk into same st, pl yarn thr, yo and pl thr 2 lps (3 lps on hk), yo, insert hk into same st, pl yarn thr, yo and pl thr 2 lps (4 lps on hk), yo and pl thr all lps.
Bobble row 1 (BR1): Sc 7, *3-dcB, sc 7, rep from *across. Turn.

Bobble row 2 (BR2): Sc 3, 3-dcB, *sc 7, 3-dcB, rep from *to last 3 sts, sc 3. Turn.

Notes:
- *BRs are worked with WS facing.*
- *Dc rows are worked with RS facing.*
- *Ch 3 at beg of row counts as a dc and first st.*

INSTRUCTIONS:

Row 1: With Color A, ch 145, dc in 4th ch and each ch across. Turn. (143 dc.)
Row 2: Ch 1, sc in each st across, end in tch. Turn.
Row 3: Ch 3 (counts as first dc), dc in each sc. Turn.
Row 4: With Color B, fol BR1, drop Color B. Turn.
Row 5: With Color A, ch 3 and dc in each st across. Turn.
Rows 6–7: Rep Rows 2–3, drop Color A. Turn.
Row 8: With Color C, fol BR2. Turn.
Rows 9–11: Rep Rows 1–3.
Row 12: With Color D, rep Row 4.
Rows 13–15: Rep Rows 1–3.
Row 16: With Color E, rep Row 8.
Rows 17–19: Rep Rows 1–3.
Row 20: With Color F, rep Row 4.

Rows 21–23: Rep Rows 1–3.
Row 24: With Color B, rep Row 8.
Rows 25–27: Rep Rows 1–3.
Row 28: With Color C, rep Row 4.
Rows 29–31: Rep Rows 1–3.
Row 32: With Color D, rep Row 8.
Rows 33–35: Rep Rows 1–3.
Row 36: With Color E, rep Row 4.
Rows 37–39: Rep Rows 1–3.
Row 40: With Color F, rep Row 8.
Rows 41–46: With Color A, dc, sc, dc, sc, dc, sc.
Rows 47–49: With Color B, dc, BR1, dc.
Row 50: With Color A, sc
Rows 51–53: With Color C, dc, BR2, dc.
Row 54: Rep Row 50.
Rows 55–57: With Color D, rep Rows 47–49.
Row 58: Rep Row 50.
Rows 59–61: With Color E, rep Rows 51–53.
Row 62: Rep Row 50.
Rows 63–65: With Color F, rep Rows 47–49.
Rows 66–72: With Color A, sc, dc, sc, dc, sc, dc, sc.
Rows 73–138: Mirror Rows 1–65 in reverse order, including the placement of BRs.

Edging:

Rnd 1: With RS facing and Color B, sl st in any corner st, ch 3 and dc around, placing 3 dc in each corner st, dc in end of each sc row and 2 dc in end of each dc row. End with an uneven number of sts on each side. Sl st to top of beg ch 3. Turn.

Rnd 2: Ch 1, *sc, 3-dcB in next st, rep from *around, adjusting sts if necessary so that there is a 3-dcB in each center corner st, sl st to beg sc, FO.

Growing Garden Afghan

DESIGNED BY NANCY NEHRING

Finished size: 45" x 60"

Flowers crocheted in strips simulate a summer flower garden. Each of six strips is composed of bright variegated flowers, leaves and ground. Strips are then crocheted together to assemble the afghan.

MATERIALS:

Yarn: 100% acrylic
   Color A—Variegated (20 oz.)
   Color B—Lime (10 oz.)
   Color C—Coffee (16 oz.)
Crochet hook: size H

SPECIFICS:

Gauge: horizontal in dc 12 dc=4"

Basic stitches used: bk lp, ch, dc, dtr, sc, sl st, trc

INSTRUCTIONS:

(Make six strips.)

Flowers:

Rnd 1: With Color A and working in bottom lp of chs [ch 16, sk 2 chs, sc, dc, 3 tr, dc, sc, ch 9, sk 2 chs, sc, dc, 3 tr, dc, sc] nineteen times, ch 9, sk 2 chs, sc, dc, 3 tr, dc, sc, working bk along other side of chs [(ch 9, sk 2 chs, sc, dc, 3 tr, dc, sc) twice, in 7 unused chs made in first half of row (sc, dc, 3 tr, dc, sc)] rep to end of row. FO.

Leaves:

Rnd 2: With Color B and working in bk lp only throughout rnd, attach yarn thr tips of two petals from adjacent flowers, ch 1 [dc in sc of petal, trc in dc and first trc of petal, ch 3, trc in first trc and dc of next petal, dc in sc of petal, sc thr tip of this petal and next petal tog] rep around except over three petals at each end of row [beg in 2 tr, dc, sc in tip, dc, tr, dtr,] ch 3, in next petal dtr, tr, dc, sc in tip, dc, tr, dtr, in next petal dtr, tr, dc, sc in tip, dc, 2 tr. Sl st into first sc. FO.

Ground:

Rnd 3: With Color C and working in bk lp only throughout rnd, attach yarn to side. Dc in each st around except over three single petals at each end work 2 dc above each petal tip and 2 dc in center of ch of the two ch 3 bet these petals (inc 5 sts on each end). Sl st to join.

Rnd 4: Cont with Color C and working in bk lp only. Ch 3 (counts as first dc), dc in each st around expect make 2 dc in each inc st of Rnd 3. Sl st to join. FO.

Assemble strips: With Color C, hold two strips WS tog. Beg above last leaf st of single petal, sc thr tops of dc of both strips tog to same point on other end of strips. Rep to join all strips.

Edging: With Color A, sc in each dc along edges and around scallops. FO.

Love Afghan

DESIGNED BY MARTY MILLER

Finished size: 30" x 22"

Bright colors and bold shapes bring life to this afghan made of simple a squares separate the "Love" squares spelling out the word love with unique geometric shapes.

MATERIALS:

Yarn: 100% acrylic, worsted weight

  Color A—Blue (5 oz.)
  Color B—Green (5 oz.)
  Color C—Lime (10 oz.)
  Color D—Orange (10 oz.)
  Color E—Orchid (5 oz.)
  Color F—Pink (5 oz.)
  Color G—Red (5 oz.)
  Color H—Turquoise (10 oz.)
  Color I—Yellow (5 oz.)

Crochet hook: size I

SPECIFICS:

Gauges: 6 sc=2"; 7 rows=2"

Basic stitches used: sc, sl st

Notes:

* *When chg colors in a row, when making the last st with old color, pl last lp thr with new color. Do not work over old color yarn. Bring yarn around to front to use later.*
* *Mark 2nd row of each square as the RS.*

INSTRUCTIONS:

Solid color square: (Make 10, one of each of the nine colors, and one extra Color C.)
Ch 31.
Row 1: Sc in 2nd ch from hk and in each ch across. [30 sc] ch 1. Turn.
Row 2: Sc in first sc and in each sc across. Ch 1. Turn.
Rows 3–36: Rep Row 2. FO.

"L" square: (Make 10.)
With Color C, ch 16.
Row 1: Sc in 2nd ch from hk and in each ch across. (15 sc.)
Row 2: Sc in first sc and in each sc across. Ch 1. Turn.
Rows 3–10: Rep Row 2.
Row 11: Sc in first 9 sc. Chg to Color E. Sc in last 6 sc. Ch 1. Turn.
Row 12: With Color E, sc in first 6 sc. Chg to Color C. Sc in last 9 sc. Ch 1. Turn.
Rows 13–18: Rep Rows 11–12 three more times. FO.

"E" square: (Make 10.)
With Color A, ch 16.
Row 1: Sc in 2nd ch from hk and in each ch across. (15 sc.)
Row 2: Sc in first sc and in each sc across. Ch 1. Turn.
Rows 3–8: Rep Row 2. Chg to Color I. Ch 1. Turn.
Rows 9–14: Rep Row 2. Chg to

Color F. Ch 1. Turn.
Rows 15–18: Rep Row 2. FO.

"0" square: (Make 10.)
With Color D, ch 16.
Row 1: Sc in 2nd ch from hk and in each ch across. (15 sc.)
Row 2: Sc in next 7 sc. Chg to Color B. Sc in next sc. Chg to Color D. Sc in next 7 sc. Ch 1. Turn.
Row 3: Sc in next 6 sc. Chg to Color B. Sc in next 3 sc. Chg to Color D. Sc in next 6 sc. Ch 1. Turn.
Row 4: Sc in next 5 sc. Chg to Color B. Sc in next 5 sc. Chg to Color D. Sc in next 5 sc. Ch 1. Turn.
Row 5: Sc in next 4 sc. Chg to Color B. Sc in next 7 sc. Chg to Color D. Sc in next 4 sc. Ch 1. Turn.
Row 6: Sc in next 3 sc. Chg to Color B. Sc in next 9 sc. Chg to Color D. Sc in next 3 sc. Ch 1. Turn.
Row 7: Sc in next 2 sc. Chg to Color B. Sc in next 11 sc. Chg to Color D. Sc in next 2 sc. Ch 1. Turn.
Row 8: Sc in next sc. Chg to Color B. Sc in next 13 sc. Chg to Color D. Sc in next sc. Chg to Color B. Ch 1. Turn.
Row 9: Sc in 15 sc. Ch 1. Turn.
Row 10: Sc in 15 sc. Chg to Color D. Ch 1. Turn.
Row 11: Sc in next sc. Chg to Color B. Sc in next 13 sc. Chg to

Continued on page 58

Continued from page 56

Color D. Sc in next sc. Ch 1. Turn.

Row 12: Sc in next 2 sc. Chg to Color B. Sc in next 11 sc. Chg to Color D. Sc in next 2 sc. Ch 1. Turn.

Row 13: Sc in next 3 sc. Chg to Color B. Sc in next 9 sc. Chg to Color D. Sc in next 3 sc. Ch 1. Turn.

Row 14: Sc in next 4 sc. Chg to Color B. Sc in next 7 sc. Chg to Color D. Sc in next 4 sc. Ch 1. Turn.

Row 15: Sc in next 5 sc. Chg to Color B. Sc in next 5 sc. Chg to Color D. Sc in next 5 sc. Ch 1. Turn.

Row 16: Sc in next 6 sc. Chg to Color B. Sc in next 3 sc. Chg to Color D. Sc in next 6 sc. Ch 1. Turn.

Row 17: Sc in next 7 sc. Chg to Color B. Sc in next sc. Chg to Color D. Sc in next 7 sc. Ch 1. Turn.

Row 18: Sc in 15 sc. FO.

"V" square: (Make 10.)
With Color H, ch 16.

Row 1: Sc in 2nd ch from hk and in each ch across. (15 sc.)

Row 2: Sc in next 7 sc. Chg to Color G. Sc in next sc. Chg to Color H. Sc in next 7 sc. Ch 1. Turn.

Row 3: Sc in next 6 sc. Chg to Color G. Sc in next 3 sc. Chg to Color H. Sc in next 6 sc. Ch 1. Turn.

Row 4: Sc in next 5 sc. Chg to Color G. Sc in next 5 sc. Chg to Color H. Sc in next 5 sc. Ch 1. Turn.

Row 5: Sc in next 4 sc. Chg to Color G. Sc in next 7 sc. Chg to Color H. Sc in next 4 sc. Ch 1. Turn.

Row 6: Sc in next 3 sc. Chg to Color G. Sc in next 9 sc. Chg to

Color H. Sc in next 3 sc. Ch 1. Turn.

Row 7: Sc in next 2 sc. Chg to Color G. Sc in next 11 sc. Chg to Color H. Sc in next 2 sc. Ch 1, turn.

Row 8: Sc in next sc. Chg to Color G. Sc in next 13 sc. Chg to Color H. Sc in next sc. Chg to Color G. Ch 1. Turn.

Rows 9–13: Sc in 15 sc. Ch 1. Turn.

Row 14: Sc in 7 sc. Chg to Color H. Sc in next sc. Chg to Color G. Sc in next 7 sc. Chg to Color H. Ch 1. Turn.

Row 15: Sc in first sc. Chg to Color G. Sc in next 5 sc. Chg to Color H, Sc in next 3 sc. Chg to Color G. Sc in next 5 sc. Chg to Color H. Sc in next sc. Ch 1. Turn.

Row 16: Sc in 2 sc. Chg to Color G. Sc in next 3 sc. Chg to Color H. Sc in next 5 sc. Chg to Color G. Sc in next 3 sc. Chg to Color H. Sc in next 2 sc. Ch 1. Turn.

Row 17: Sc in next 4 sc. Chg to Color G. Sc in next sc. Chg to Color H, Sc in next 5 sc. Chg to Color G. Sc in next sc. Chg to Color H. Sc in next 4 sc. Ch 1. Turn.

Row 18: Sc in 15 sc. FO.

Construction: Sew squares tog to form large square. With WS facing, sew "L" and "V" squares tog using Color C. Join by sewing thr bottom of Color C ch on the "L" square and the bk lp of the Color H scs on the "V" square. With WS facing, sew "O" and "E" squares tog using Color E. Join by sewing thr bottom of Color D ch on "O" square and bk lp of Color E scs on

"E" square. With RS facing, join two strips tog to form a large square, using Color D to sew upper two squares and Color H to sew lower two squares tog. Arrange all squares as shown in Placement of squares diagram. Sew squares in each column tog with WS facing, using yarn matching one of the adjacent solid color squares. Catch only bk lps of the scs. Sew columns to each other with RS facing, using yarn matching adjacent solid color square.

Edging:

Row 1: Join Color D in any corner. Three sc in same corner st. Sc in each sc across top and bottom, and in each row along sides, making 3 sc in each corner. Join with a sl st to the first sc. End Color D, and join Color H.

Row 2: Sc in each sc around, making 3 sc in each corner. Join with sl st to the first sc. End Color H.

Rows 3–9: Rep Row 2 using the fol colors: Color G, Color I, Color E, Color B, Color F, Color A, Color C. FO. Weave in ends.

LOVE Construction diagrams

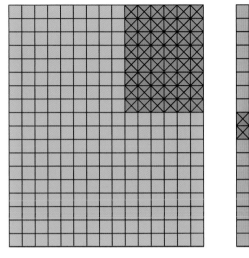

"L" square

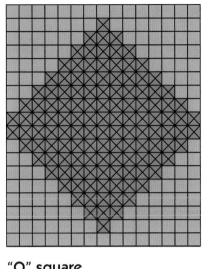

"O" square

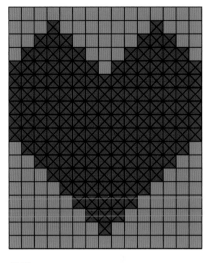

"V" square

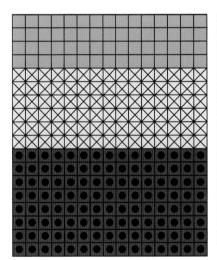

"E" square

LOVE square

Placement of squares

59

Take 'n Make Afghan

DESIGNED BY ROBERTA J. GARDNER

Finished size: 44" x 66"

This afghan is made in 4" strips that are portable and easy to carry along to work on whenever you find yourself waiting in lines, at stoplights, in offices or at ball games.

MATERIALS:

Yarn: worsted weight
Color A—Amethyst (24 oz.)
Color B—Forest Green (6 oz.)
Color C—Gemstone (24 oz.)
Crochet hook: size L

SPECIFICS:

Gauges: 7 sts=2"; 6 rows=2"

Basic stitches used: ch, sc, sl st

Notes:

- *To create zigzag patt in gemstone strips, start each strip at same color rep in the skein.*
- *Each skein should have the colorway repeated in the same sequence and in the same six lengths of 22", 16", 48", 16", 48", and 16".*
- *Size of afghan can be chg by varying size and/or number of strips.*

INSTRUCTIONS:

Strips:

Rows 1–133: Ch 15, sc in 3rd ch from hk. *Ch 1, sk 1 ch and sc in next ch*. Rep across end in top of ch 2 turning st.; 7 sc and 6 ch 1 sps. *Ch 2. Turn. Sc in first ch 1 sp, ch 1 and sc in each ch 1 sp across end in top of ch 2 turning st*. Rep until you have 133 rows or strip measures 44". Make eight Color A strips and seven Color C strips.

Assembly: Align bottom edges of a Color A strip and a Color C strip with WS tog and attach Color B in bottom row with a sl st. Sc in next st, *ch 1, sk 1 st and sc in next *. Rep to top of strips, cut yarn and weave in ends. Rep alternating colors until all strips are joined.

Edging: Attach Color B yarn at any outside point with a sl st and *ch 1 , sk 1 sc and sc in next st *. Rep all around afghan. Put 3 sc in each corner so it will lay flat. Aft completing Color B edge, join with a sl st, cut yarn and FO. Weave in ends.

Rainbow Blocks Afghan

DESIGNED BY RUTHIE MARKS

Finished size: 46" x 69"

Alternating back loop and front loop half double crochet stitches, keep the pattern stitch throughout, even when changing colors.

MATERIALS:

Yarn: 100% acrylic, worsted weight:
  Color A—Red (9 oz.)
  Color B—Orange (9 oz.)
  Color C—Yellow (9 oz.)
  Color D—Green (9 oz.)
  Color E—Blue (9 oz.)
  Color F—Violet (9 oz.)
Crochet hooks: sizes J, K

SPECIFICS:

Gauge: 7 hdc and 5 rows=2"

Basic stitches used: hdc, sc, sl st

Notes:
- *To chg colors, complete hdc to last step (3 hdc on hk), drop first color and pl 2nd color thr to complete st as usual. Always drop colors not in use to WS of work.*
- *To chg colors with a sl st: insert hk into next st, drop color, pick up next color and pl thr to complete sl st.*
- *Ch 2 at beg of rows does not count as a st.*
- *All edge sides are worked independently, then joined as final step.*

INSTRUCTIONS:

With J hk and Color F, ch 146.
Row 1: (WS) Hdc in 3rd ch from hk (counts as first hdc) and next 71 ch, pl ends toward you (this is the WS), drop Color F; with Color E, hdc in next 72 sts. Turn. (144 hdc)
Row 2: Ch 2 (does not count as a st), hdc in next 72 sts, chg to Color F, hdc in next 72 sts. Turn.
Rows 3–216: Follow chart, chg colors where indicated, keeping in patt st at all times. Work in all ends.

Continued on page 64

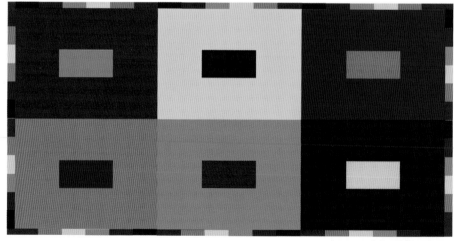

Assembly Diagram

Continued from page 63

Edging:

Rnd 1: (WS) Starting with Color E in unused beg lp of foundation ch, sc in first st, sc to end of Color E blk (72 sts), chg to Color F, sc to end of Color F blk (72 sts), sc 72 sts evenly sp up side of afghan to end of Color F blk; cont around afghan, matching colors as they chg and working thr both lps across top (72 sts for each color on all edges). FO.

Row 1: With K hk and Color A, ch 10. Hdc in 3rd ch from hk and in next 6 ch. (8 hdc) Yo and proceed on afghan edge from any corner with patt st for 12 sts—20 hdc (first 8 sts will extend out independently from beg of row on edge of afghan). Chg to Color B, hdc in next 12 sts, chg to Color C, hdc in next 12 sts, chg to Color D, hdc in next 12 sts, chg to Color E, hdc in next 12 sts, chg to Color F, hdc in next 12 sts, chg to Color A, hdc in next 12 sts, rep from *to end of row. Turn—152 sts on short sides, 224 sts on long sides.

Row 2: Ch 2, hdc in each st, chg colors where appropriate, rep to end of row. Turn.

Rows 3–4: Rep Row 2.

Row 5: Ch 1, sl st in each st to end. Fasten off all six colors. Rep for other three sides. With Color A, sew ends of rows tog to form corners, easing to fit.**

Fish Afghan

Fish Afghan

DESIGNED BY KATHLEEN STUART

Finished size: 60" x 72"

Since this afghan is constructed of a number of individual squares, it is an easy project to work on when space is limited. The squares are worked diagonally, from corner to corner. Once the squares are connected together, an array of black button eyes and white button bubbles accentuate these fish in the sea.

MATERIALS:

Yarn: 100% acrylic
  Color A—Periwinkle (50 oz.)
  Color B—Yellow (5 oz.)
  Color C—Red (5 oz.)
  Color D—Lime (5 oz.)
Crochet hook: size J
Additional supplies:
  Buttons:
    black ½" (20)
    white or clear ⅜"–¾" (60)
  Needle and thread

SPECIFICS:

Gauges: square=8½";
  diagonal 12"

Basic stitches used: ch, dc, sc, sl st

Special stitches used:
Beginning block (Bblk): Ch 5, turn; 3 dc in 4th ch from hk.

Block (blk): Sl st in ch-3 sp of next blk, ch 3, 3 dc in same sp.

Notes:
* *When chg colors, keep unused color to WS of work; do not cut yarn until color is no longer needed.*
* *Do not carry colors on WS of work, unless otherwise noted.*
* *Use a separate ball for each chg.*

INSTRUCTIONS:

Plain square: (Make 30.)
Row 1: With Color A, ch 5, 3 dc in 5th ch from hk. (First blk.)
Row 2: Work Bblk, sl st around beg ch of prev blk, ch 3, 3 dc in same sp. (2 blks.)
Row 3: Work Bblk, sl st around beg ch of prev blk, ch 3, 3 dc in same sp, work 1 blk. (3 blks.)

Rows 4–11: Rep Row 3. (Blks 4–11.)
Row 12: Turn; sl st in first 3 dc and in first ch-3 sp, ch 3, 3 dc in same sp, work 9 blks, sl st in ch-3 sp of last blk. (10 blks.)
Rows 13–21: Rep Row 12.
Row 22 (edge rnd): Ch 1, 2 sc in same sp, sc 21 sts evenly across side of square, 3 sc in corner st, sc 25 sts evenly across next side, 3 sc in corner st, sc 25 sts evenly across next side, 3 sc in corner st, sc 25 sts evenly across next side, 3 sc in corner st, sc in last 2 sts of first side, sl st in first sc; FO.

Fish square: (Make 20: seven Color C, seven Color B, six Color D.)
Row 1: With Color B, ch 5, 3 dc in 5th ch from hk, work. (First blk.)
Row 2: Work Bblk, sl st around beg ch of prev blk, ch 3, 3 dc in same sp. (2 blks.)
Row 3: Work Bblk, sl st around beg ch of prev blk, ch 3, 3 dc in same sp, work 1 blk. (3 blks.)
Rows 4–7: Rep Row 3. (4–7 blks.)

Row 8: Work Bblk, sl st around beg ch of prev blk, ch 3, 3 dc in same sp, work 6 blks chg yarn to Color A in last st. (8 blks.)

Row 9: Work Bblk, chg yarn to Color D in last st, sl st around beg ch of prev blk, ch 3, 3 dc in same sp, work 6 blks, chg yarn to Color A in last st, work 1 blk. (9 blks.)

Row 12: Turn; sl st in first 3 dc and in first ch-3 sp, ch 3, 3 dc in same sp, chg yarn to Color D in last st, work 8 blks, chg yarn to Color A in last st, work 1 blk, sl st in ch-3 sp of last blk. (10 blks.)

Rows 13–21: Rep Row 12.

Rnd 22 (edge rnd): Ch 1, 2 sc in same sp, sc 21 sts evenly across side of square, 3 sc in corner st, sc 25 sts evenly across next side, 3 sc in corner st, sc 25 sts evenly across next side, 3 sc in corner st, sc 25 sts evenly across next side, 3 sc in corner st, sc in last 2 sts of first side, sl st in first sc; FO.

Joining: Refer to Fish Assembly Diagram. Join squares by placing RS tog and sl st in ft lp of square closest to you and bk lp of other square. Start with top right square in first row and rightmost fish square in 2nd row; cont joining first two rows in one cont line. Cont adding rows in like manner.

Edging: Join with sc in any outer corner of any outer square, [3 sc in every outer corner st, sc in every st along sides, at inner corners: sc in corner st of each of the three adjoining squares] around entire afghan, FO.

Finishing: Sew black button on 2nd blk of Row 4 for eye of each fish. Sew 2–3 white buttons onto Color A squares close to mouth of fish for bubbles.

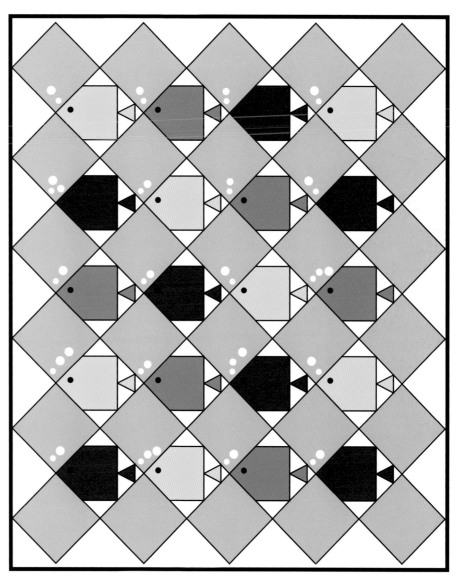

Fish Assembly Diagram

Carnival Afghan

DESIGNED BY WILLENA NANTON

Finished size: 84" x 60"

> The use of three different yarn types brings character to this festive afghan while the multiple colors bring a party flavor.

MATERIALS:

Yarn:

Color A—Hot Pink acrylic (32 oz.)

Color B—Hot Pink polar spun (3½ oz.)

Color C—Strawberry soft boucle (7½ oz.)

Color D—Hot Pink fur (8¾ oz.)

Color E—Multicolored homespun (12 oz.)

Crochet hook: size G

SPECIFICS:

Gauge: Rows 1–5=3" x 3"

Basic stitches used: dc, sc, sl st

INSTRUCTIONS:

Start with Color A, Ch 2.
Do not join rnds.

Rnd 1: 6 sc in 2nd ch from hk. (6 sts.)

Rnd 2: 2 sc in each sc around. (12 sts.)

Rnd 3: Sc in first sc, 2 sc in next sc, sc in next sc, [2 sc in next sc. Rep to end. (18 sts.)].

Rnd 4: Sc in first sc, sc in next sc, 2 sc in next sc, [sc in next sc, sc in next sc, 2 sc in next sc. Rep to end. (24 sts.)]

Notes:

- *Aft Rnd 4, join aft each rnd.*
- *To join rnds, sk st in first st made and ch 1 if next rnd starts with a sc or ch 3 if next rnd starts with dc.*

Rnd 5: Sl st in first st. Ch 3, dc in next sc, dc in next 3 sc, [2 dc, ch 2, 2 dc] in next sc, [dc in next 5 sc, (2 dc, ch 2, 2 dc in next sc) three times]. Sl st in top of ch 3. FO. (9 dc per side.)

Rnd 6: Join Color B. Sl st in sl st. Ch 1. Sc in same sc, sc in next 2 dc, [sc, ch 2, sc] in ch 2 sp, [sc in next 9 dc, (sc, ch 2, sc) in next ch 2 sp three times]. Sc in next 6 dc. Sl st in first st. (11 sc per side.)

Rnd 7: Ch 1. Sc in same st as sl st, sc in next 3 sc, [sc, ch 2, sc] in ch 2 sp, [sc in next 11 sc, (sc, ch 2, sc) in ch 2 sp three times]. Sc in next 7 sc. Join. FO. (13 sc per side)

Rnd 8: Join Color A. Ch 3, dc in next sc, dc in next 3 sc, [dc, ch 2, dc] in ch 2 sp, [dc in next 13 dc, (dc, ch 2, dc) in next ch 2 sp three times]. Dc in next 8 sc. Join. FO. (15 sc per side.)

Rnd 9: Join Color C. Ch 1. Sc in same st, sc in next 5 dc, [sc, ch 2, sc] in ch 2 sp, [sc in next 15 dc, (sc, ch 2, sc) in next ch 2 sp three times]. Sc in next 9 dc. Join. (17 sc per side.)

Rnd 10: Join. Ch 1. Sc in same sc as sl st, sc in next 6 sc, [sc, ch 2, sc] in ch 2 sp, [sc in next 17 sc, (sc, ch 2, sc) in next ch 2 sp three times]. Sc in next 10 sc. Join. (19 sc per side.)

Rnd 11: Ch 1. Sc in sl st, sc in next 7 sc, [sc, ch 2, sc] in ch 2 sp, [sc in next 19 sc, (sc, ch 2, sc) in next ch 2 sp three times]. Sc in next 11 sc. Join. (21 sc per side.) FO.

Rnd 12: Join Color A. Ch 3. Dc in next sc, dc in next 7 sc, [dc, ch 2, dc] in ch 2 sp, [dc in next 21 sc, (sc, ch 2, sc) in ch 2 sp. Rep two more times], dc in next 12 sc. Join. (23 dc per side.)

Rnd 13: Ch 1, sc in sl st, sc in next 8 sc, [sc, ch 2, sc] in ch 2 sp, [sc in next 23 sc, (sc, ch 2, sc) in next ch 2 sp three times]. Sc in next 14 sc.

Continued on page 70

Continued from page 68

Join. (25 sc per side.) FO.

Rnd 14: Join Color D. Ch 1, sc in sl st, sc in next 9 sc, (sc, ch 2, sc) in ch 2 sp, [sc in next 25 sc, (sc, ch 2, sc) in next ch 2 sp three times]. Sc in next 15 sc. Join. (27 sc per side.)

Rnd 15: Ch 1, sc in sl st, sc in next 10 sc, [sc, ch 2, sc] in ch 2 sp, [sc in next 27 sc, (sc, ch 2, sc) in next ch 2 sp three times]. Sc in next 16 sc. Join. (29 sc per side.) FO.

Rnd 16: Join Color A, ch 1, sc in sl st, sc in next 11 sc, [sc, ch 2, sc] in ch 2 sp, [sc in next 29 sc, (sc, ch 2, sc) in next ch 2 sp three times]. Sc in next 17 sc. Join. (31 sc per side.) FO.

Rnd 17: Join Color E. Ch 1, sc in sl st, sc in next 12 sc, (sc, ch 2, sc) in ch 2 sp, [sc in next 31 sc, (sc, ch 2, sc) in next ch 2 sp three times]. Sc in next 18 sc. Join. (33 sc per side.)

Rnd 18: Ch 3, dc in next sc, dc in next 12 sc, (dc, ch 2, dc) in ch 2 sp, [dc in next 19 sc, (dc, ch 2, dc) in next ch 2 sp three times]. Dc in next 19 sc. Join. (35 dc per side.) FO.

Rnd 19: Join Color A. Ch 1, sc in sl st, sc in next 14 dc, [sc, ch 2, sc] in ch 2 sp, [sc in next 35 dc, (sc, ch 2, sc) in next ch 2 sp three times]. Sc in next 20 dc. Join. (37 sc per side.) FO.

Assembly: With Color A and RS tog, sc in bk lps of each square from corner to corner and FO. Join four squares wide; six sets of four squares each.

Top Border: With Color A. Complete border six times on top row of sets. Complete top border on bottom row of one of the sets. One set will have top border twice. Working in sts of each set.

Row 1: Sc in each st across and in connecting sp of squares place one sc. Turn.

Row 2: Ch 3, sk first sc, dc in next sc, dc in each sc across. FO.

Bottom border: Join with Color A. Complete border five times on bottom row of the sets. Working on bottom row of each set.

Row 1: Sc in each st across and in connecting sp of squares place 1 sc. FO.

Assembly: Join with Color A. Join sets to each other. Place double top row on bottom. Then connect top to bottom rows. With RS tog, sc in bk lps of each st. FO. Join sets, which will equal four squares wide and six squares long.

Edging: Join with Color A, but do not start in a corner sp.

Rnd 1: Sc in each st across. In corner sp [sc, ch 2, sc]. In connecting square sp, place 6 sc evenly in sides of sts. Join.

Rnd 2: Ch 3, sk first dc, dc in next dc, dc in each sc around. In corner sp [dc, ch 2, dc]. Join. FO.

Rnd 3: Join with Color B. Ch 1, sc in same sp as sl st, sc in next dc, sc in each dc around. In corner sp [sc, ch 2, sc]. Join. FO.

Rnd 4: Join with Color A. Ch 1, sc in same sp as sl st, sc in next dc, sc in each dc around. In corner sp [sc, ch 2, sc]. Join. FO.

Rnd 5: Join with Color E. Ch 3, sk first dc, dc in next dc, dc in each sc around. In corner sp [dc, ch 2, dc]. Join. FO.

Rnd 6: Join with Color A. Ch 1, sc in same sp as sl st, sc in next dc, sc in each dc around. In corner sp [sc, ch 2, sc]. Join. FO. Weave in loose ends.

Sophisticated Ele

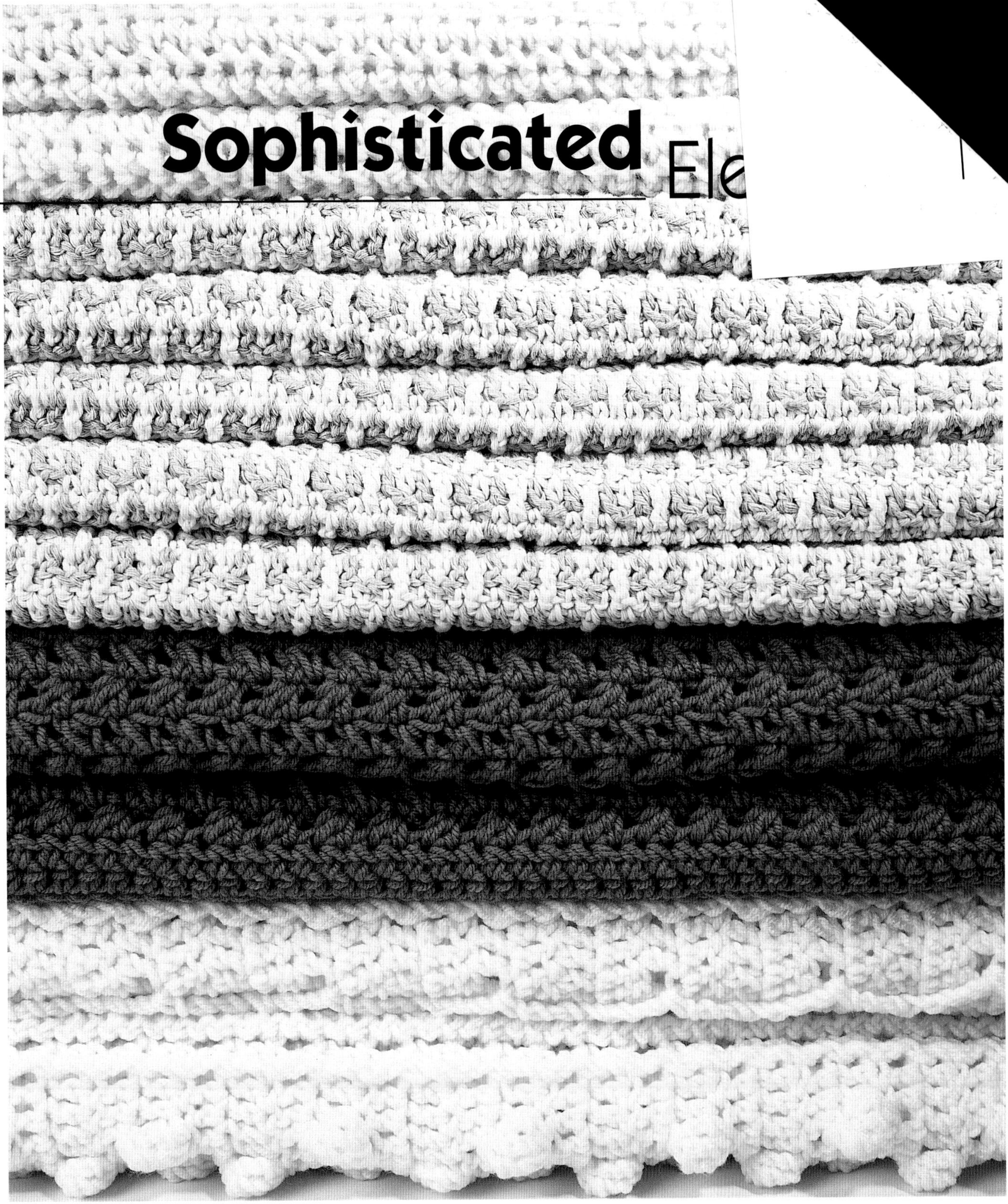

Light Plum Afghan

DESIGNED BY RUTHIE MARKS

Finished size: 45" x 57"

The lacy border of this afghan surrounds the soft texture of cluster stitches. Using a single color accentuates the beauty of the patterned clusters and stitches.

MATERIALS:

Yarn: 100% acrylic
Light Plum (40 oz.)
Crochet hooks: sizes J, K
Additional supplies:
Tapestry needle

SPECIFICS:

Gauge: With K hk, 8 hdc + 6 CL rows=3"

Basic stitches used: dc, hdc, sc, sl st

Special stitch used:

Half double crochet cluster (hdcCL): Yo, insert hk in first st and pl lp thr (3 lps on hk), yo, insert hk in 2nd st and pl lp thr (5 lps on hk), yo and pl thr all lps.

INSTRUCTIONS:

Row 1: With K hk, ch 121. Hdc in 2nd ch from hk and each ch across. Turn. (120 hdc.)

Rows 2–3: Ch 2 (counts as first hdc), hdc in 2nd hdc and each hdc across. Turn.

Row 4: Ch 2, hdcCL in first 2 sts, *ch 1, hdcCL in next 2 sts, rep from *across to last 2 sts, end last hdcCL in tch. Turn. (60 hdcCL.)

Row 5: Ch 2, hdcCL beg in first 5-lp sp (first horizontal st) and ch-1 sp (looks like an "eye"), *ch 1, hdcCL in next 2 sts, rep from *across, end last hdcCL in tch. Turn.

Rows 6–10: Rep Row 5.

Rows 11–13: Ch 2 (counts as first hdc), hdc in each st across, end last hdc in tch. Turn.

Row 14: Rep Row 4.

Rows 15–20: Rep Row 5.

Rows 21–110: Rep Rows 11–20 nine times.

Rows 111–113: Rep Row 5. Turn. Do not FO.

Edging:

Rnd 1: With J hk, 3 sc in corner st, 120 sc across, 3 sc in corner st, 160 sc down one side, 3 sc in corner st, 120 sc across, 3 sc in corner st, 160 sc up other side, sl st to beg sc. Turn.

Rnd 2: Ch 3 (counts as first st), dc in next 3 sts, ch 2, sk 2 sts, *dc in next 3 sts, ch 2, sk 2 sts, rep from *to last 4 sts bef the corner st, dc in next 4 sts, ch 2, dc in corner st, ch 2, [dc in next 4 sts, ch 2, sk 2 sts, dc in next 3 sts, ch 2, sk 2 sts, rep to last 4 sts bef the corner st, dc in next 4 sts, ch 2, dc in corner st, ch 2] three times, sl st to beg ch 3. FO. Turn.

Rnd 3: Join with a sc in first dc aft any corner st, *ch 3, sk next dc, dc in next dc, ch 3, sk next dc, sc in ch-2 sp, ch 3, sk next dc, dc in next dc, ch 3, sk next dc, sc in ch-2 sp, rep from *to last 4 dc, (ch 3, sk next dc, dc in next dc, ch 3, sk next dc, sc in next dc, ch 4, dc in corner dc, ch 4, sc in next dc, rep from beg *around, sl st to beg sc. FO.

Cool Cotton Throw

DESIGNED BY AMY BREWER

Finished size: 42" x 55"

This throw works two rows on the same side before turning, which enables you to change colors every row without cutting. The woven appearance comes from using a double crocheted mesh, followed by a row of treble crochet alternately worked in front of and behind the previous rows' spaces.

MATERIALS:

Yarn: 75% cotton/25% acrylic
  Color A—White (1600 yds.)
  Color B—Linen (1200 yds.)
Crochet hook: size G
Additional supplies:
  Safety pin
  Yarn needle

SPECIFICS:

Gauges: ch 22=5";
  first 9 rows=3"

Basic stitches used: ch, sl st, sc, dc, tr

INSTRUCTIONS:

Multiple of 4 + 2. With Color A ch 174.

Row 1: (RS) Sc in 2nd ch from hk and in each ch across chg to Color B in last sc.
Row 2: Ch 3. Turn. Dc in 2nd st, [ch 1, sk next st, dc in next st] across. Dc in last st. Do not turn. Drop Color B and secure with safety pin. Draw up a lp of Color A thr 3rd ch of beg ch 3.
Row 3: Ch 1, sc in first 2 sts, *working behind next ch 1, trc in next sk sc 2 rows down, sc in next dc, working in front of next ch 1, trc in next sk sc 2 rows down, sc in next dc *, rep bet *s across. Sc in last st drawing up a lp of Color B and dropping Color A. Rep Rows 2 and 3 until body measures 54" long. At end, cut Color A leaving a 6" length

for weaving. Be certain to not cut Color B.

Edging:

Rnd 1: With Color B ch 1. Turn. Work 2 sc in first st, sc in each st across, 2 sc in last st. Working down side, *[2 sc in ends of dc rows, 1 sc in end of sc row] across **. Working in free lps of beg ch, 2 sc in first lp, sc in each lp across, 2 sc in last lp. Working up other side, rep from *to **. Join with sl st in first sc.
Rnd 2: Sl st to next st, ch 1 *[sc, ch 2, dc] in next st, **sk next st, rep from *across to first corner st end at **. Rep from *around.
Sl st in first sc to join. Using yarn needle, weave in loose ends.

Lacy Lattice Afghan

DESIGNED BY JANET REHFELDT & CAROL LYKINS

Finished size: 52" x 72" with border

This afghan is worked lengthwise using a revised Persian stitch for a lacy crossed-lattice look. The beautifully slanted edging is worked using front post treble crochet stitches.

MATERIALS:

Yarn: worsted weight
Color A—Off-white (48 oz.)
Crochet hooks: sizes I, L

SPECIFICS:

Gauge: 11 sts x 8 rows=4"
in patt st

Basic stitches used: hdc, sc, sl st

Special stitch used:

Front post slant treble crochet (FPstr): First rnd of border: yo hk twice, insert hk around post from front to bk of sk hdc in row below, draw up a lp, yo and draw thr 2 lps on hk three times. Do not work or count st directly behind FPstr just made. On all fol rnds of the border, work FPstr around prev FPstr st.

INSTRUCTIONS:

Row 1: With size L hk, ch 193, working in bottom lp of ch, sc in 2nd ch from hk, sc in each ch across. Turn. (192 sc.)

Row 2: (RS) Ch1, insert hk into bk lp of first st, yo, pl up a lp, insert hk into ft lp of same st, yo, pl up a lp, yo, draw thr 3 lps on hk, *insert hk into base of last st just made, yo, draw up a lp, insert hk into next st, yo, draw up a lp (3 lps on hk), yo, draw thr all lps on hk *rep from *to *across. Turn. (192 sts.) Rep Row 2 until piece measures approx 49" from beg end with a RS. Do not turn. Do not FO.

Slanted post stitch border:

Rnd 1: (RS) Using size I hk, ch 1, 3 sc in last st made on afghan body, (counts as first corner), work 352 sc sts evenly sp as fol; 190 sc sts along side edges and 150 sts along top and bottom working 3 sc in each corner, sl st in first ch 1 to close rnd.

Rnd 2: Ch 2 (counts as first hdc), hdc in each dc, working 3 hdc in corners, join with sl st in top of first ch 2.

Rnd 3: Ch 2 (counts as first hdc), sk 1 hdc, sc in next hdc, *FPstr around sk hdc (yo hk twice, insert hk from front to bk around post of the sk hdc, draw up a lp, yo and draw thr 2 lps on hk three times), **sk 1 hdc, sc in next hdc *rep from *to *to within 3 corner sts end at ** (hdc in each of the next 2 hdc, 3 hdc in the corner hdc, 1 hdc in next hdc, sk 1 hdc, sc in next hdc) rep from *around, sl st in top of ch 2. FO.

Rnd 4: Rep Rnd 3.

Rnd 5: Ch 2 (counts as first hdc), sk 1 hdc, sc in next hdc, *FPstr around prev FPstr 2 rnds below **sk 1 hdc, sc in next hdc, *rep from *to *to within 3 corner sts end at ** (hdc in each of the next 2 hdc, 3 hdc in the corner hdc, 2 hdc in next hdc, sk 1 hdc, sc in next hdc, FPstr around sk hdc) [slant treble inc made] rep from *around, sl st in top of beg. Ch 2. FO.

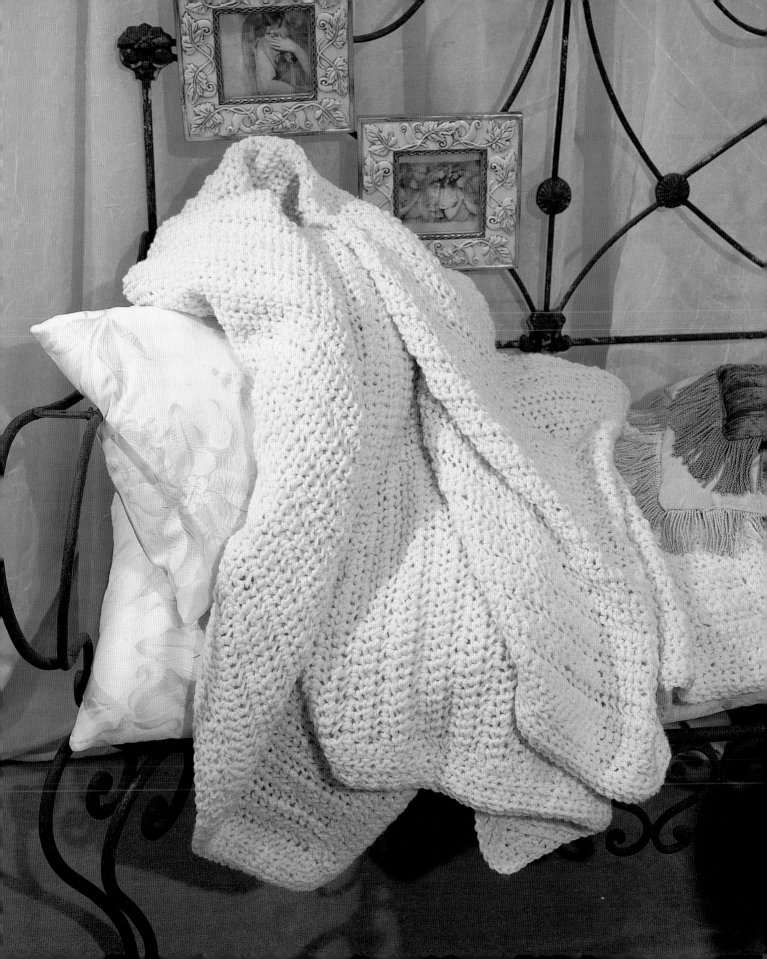

Aran Afghan

DESIGNED BY NANCY NEHRING

Finished size: 45" x 80"

This aran (fisherman) style afghan is rich in texture. Crochet is simplified with each textured pattern worked as an individual panel. It is composed of seven panels: one center double diamond pattern and two each of bars, bobbles, and basket-weave. The panels are crocheted together. This pattern can be increased or decreased in length by multiples of four rows.

MATERIALS:

Yarn: 100% acrylic
   White (55 oz.)
Crochet hook: size H

SPECIFICS:

Gauge: dc=12 sts/4"

Basic stitches used: ch, dc, trc

Special stitches used:

Back post double crochet (BPdc): Place dc around post of st in row below, going from bk to front and around to bk again. Finish dc as usual.

Front post double crochet (FPdc): Start dc around post of st in row below, going from front to bk and around to front again. Finish dc as usual. Ch 2 at beg of row counts as FPdc. Hdc at end of row counts as FPdc.

Front post double treble cluster (FPdtrCL): Wrap yarn around hk four times, insert hk around 2nd FPdtr 2 rows below, [yo, work off 2 lps] three times, retain last lp on hk, wrap yarn around hk four times, insert hk around 3rd FPdtr 2 rows below, [yo, work off 2 lps] three times, yo, pl thr all rem lps on hk.

Treble crochet cluster (trcCL): Working all 5 trc in same st [wrap yarn around hk three times, insert hk thr st below, yo, work off 2 lps, yo, work off 2 lps, retain last lp on hk] five times, yo, pl thr all lps on hk, ch 1. Count next row to be certain you have correct number of sts. When working next row, work 2 sts in the CL instead of just one.

INSTRUCTIONS:

Double diamond pattern:
(Make one.) Place FPdtr around st 2 rows below. Sk dc in row below when making a FPdtr or FPdtrCL. Ch 20.

Row 1: Ch 3 (counts as first dc), dc across. Turn. (21 sts.)

Row 2: Ch 3, dc, BPdc, 15 dc, BPdc, dc, dc in tch. Turn.

Row 3: Ch 3, dc, FPdc, 2 dc, FPdtr around 8th st 2 rows below, 2 dc, FPdtr around 11th st 2 rows below, dc, trcCL, dc, FPdtr around 11th st 2 rows below again, 2 dc, FPdtr around 4th st 2 rows below, 2 dc, FPdc, dc, dc in tch. Turn.

Row 4: Ch 3, dc, BPdc, 15 dc, BPdc, dc, dc in tch. Turn.

Row 5: Ch 3, dc, FPdc, 4 dc, FPdtr around first FPdtr, 2 dc, FPdtr cl, 2 dc, FPdtr around 4th FPdtr, 4 dc, FPdc, dc, dc in tch. Turn.

Row 6: Ch 3, dc, BPdc, 15 dc, BPdc, dc, dc in tch. Turn.

Row 7: Ch 3, dc, FPdc, 2 dc, FPdtr around first FPdtr, 2 dc, FPdtr around 2nd and 3rd FPdtr, dc, trcCL, dc, FPdtr around 2nd and 3rd FPdtr again, 2 dc, FPdtr around 4th FPdtr, 2 dc, FPdc, dc, dc in tch.

Rows 8–132: Rep Rows 4–7 until there are 33 diamonds. End with Row 5.

Continued on page 80

Continued from page 78

Bar pattern (Make two.)

Ch 19.

Row 1: (WS) Ch 3 (counts as first dc), dc across. Turn. (20 sts.)

Row 2: Ch 3, dc, FPdc, 14 BLtrc (this is trc not dc), FPdc, dc, dc in tch. Turn.

Row 3: Ch 3, dc, BPdc, 14 dc, BPdc, dc, dc in tch.

Rows 4–132: Rep Rows 2–3.

Bobble pattern: (Make two.)

Ch 14.

Row 1: (WS) Ch 3, (counts as first dc), dc across. Turn. (15 sts.)

Row 2: Ch 3, dc, FPdc, 2 dc, trcCl, 3 dc, trcCl, 2 dc, FPdc, dc, dc in tch. Turn.

Rows 3 and 5: Ch 3, dc, BPdc, 9 dc, BPdc, dc, dc in tch. Turn.

Row 4: Ch 3, dc, FPdc, 4 dc, trcCl, 4 dc, FPdc, dc, dc in tch.

Rows 5–132: Rep Rows 2–5.

Basket-weave Pattern: (Make two.) Ch 25.

Row 1: Ch 3 (counts as first dc), dc across. Turn. (26 sts.)

Row 2: Ch 3, dc, FPdc, [4 BPtrc, 4 FPtrc] twice, 4 BPtrc, FPdc, dc, dc in tch. Turn.

Row 3: Ch 3, dc, BPdc, [4 FPtrc, 4 BPtrc] twice, 4 FPtrc, BPdc, dc, dc in tch. Turn.

Row 4: Ch 3: dc, FPdc, [4 FPtrc, 4 BPtrc] twice, 4 FPtrc, FPdc, dc, dc in tch. Turn.

Row 5: Ch 3, dc, BPdc, [4 BPtrc, 4 FPtrc] twice, 4 BPtrc, BPdc, dc, dc in tch. Turn.

Rows 6–132: Rep Rows 2–5.

Finish:

Arrange sections: Basket-weave, bobble, bar, double diamond, bar, bobble, basket-weave. To join sections, hold sections WS tog, work [sl st around bar, ch 1] twice over each pair of dc bars along long sides. Attach yarn to edge. Work one sc in each end st. Along sides, work 1 sc where rows join and 2 scs over each dc post or as needed to keep edge flat. Work 3 scs in each corner.

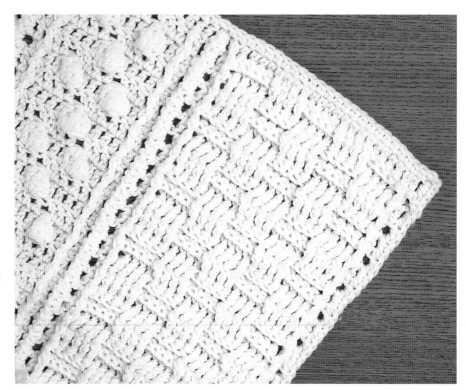

Warm & Cozy

Colorful Squares Afghan

DESIGNED BY DELMA MYERS

Finished size: 48" x 63"

> All the inner squares in this afghan are made identically. When sewing them together they are turned to create the stacked design. The solid-colored border unites the squares.

MATERIALS:

Yarn: worsted weight
    Color A—Variegated (23 oz.)
    Color B—Light Plum (14 oz.)
    Color C—Light Sage (14 oz.)
    Color D—Frosty Green (4 oz.)
Crochet hook: size G
Additional supplies:
    Tapestry needle

SPECIFICS:

Gauges: 3½ sts=1"; square=7½"
Basic stitches used: ch, dc, sl st

Notes:
- *Ch 3 at beg of a row counts as a dc.*
- *When starting or end yarn, leave 8" tail for sewing squares tog.*
- *To sew squares tog, place two squares edge to edge. Use tails in matching colors. Sew st in each square alternately.*

INSTRUCTIONS:

Square 1: (Make 24.)
With Color A, ch 4, sl st in first ch to form a ring.
Row 1: Ch 3, dc in ring, ch 3, 2 dc in ring. Turn. (4 dc.)
Row 2: Ch 3, dc in dc [2 dc, ch 3, 2 dc] in ch sp (corner), dc in 2 dc. Turn. (8 dc.)
Row 3: Ch 3, dc to corner, [2 dc, ch 3, 2 dc] in corner, dc in each dc to end. Turn. (12 dc.)
Row 4: Ch 3, dc in dc [2 dc, ch 3, 2 dc] in corner, dc to end. Turn. (16 dc.)
Rows 5–10: Cont inc 4 dc per row. At end of Row 10, FO. Turn. (40 dc in Row 10.)
Row 11: Attach Color B to first dc, ch 3, dc in each dc to corner [2 dc, ch 3, 2 dc] in corner, dc to end. Turn.
Rows 12–13: Cont inc 4 dc per row. FO.

Square 2: (Make 24.)
Rep Square 1 to Row 11. Attach Color C and cont as for Square 1.

Assembling squares:

Row A: (Make four.)
Sew six squares tog alternating Squares 1 and 2. Solid color rows should be on left and bottom sides.
Row B: (Make four.)
Sew six squares tog alternating Squares 2 and 1. Solid color rows should be on left and bottom sides. Sew eight rows tog alternating Rows A and B.

Edging:

Row 1: Attach Color D in a corner sp. Ch 3, dc in corner, dc in each dc to next corner *[2 dc, ch 3, 2 dc] in corner, dc in each dc to corner *. Rep bet *three times, [2 dc, ch 3] in corner, sl st to top of ch 3. FO. Turn.
Row 2: Attach Color C in a corner and rep edge Row 1. FO. Turn.
Row 3: Attach Color B in any corner. Rep edge Row 1. FO.

Colorful Assembly Diagram

Linked Quads Afghan

DESIGNED BY RUTHIE MARKS

Finished size: 41" x 58"

A bold design is created with a mixture of thin stripes, a wide border, a solid center, and loose stitches.

MATERIALS:

Yarn: 100% acrylic
Color A—Dark Pastel
   Variegated (40 oz.)
Color B—Periwinkle (8 oz.)
Color C—Frosty Green (8 oz.)
Crochet hook: size K
Additional supplies:
   Tapestry needle

SPECIFICS:

Gauge: 6 sc and 1 Lqtr=2"

Basic stitches used: dc, sc

Special stitches used:

Linked quadruple treble (Lqtr):
Any number of sts plus 6 for foundation ch. Insert hk down thr upper of 5 horizontal lps around stem of last st, yo, draw lp thr, insert hk down thr next horizontal lp and draw lp thr, rep until 6 lps on hk, insert hk normally into next st, yo, draw lp thr st (7 lps on hk), [yo, draw thr 2 lps] six times. To make Lqtr at beg of row, ch 6, insert hk into 2nd, 3rd, 4th, 5th, and 6th chs from hk, sk first st,

insert hk in next st and complete st as usual. Two Lqtr completed. (Ch-6 counts as first Lqtr.)

Double crochet cluster (dcCL1):
multiple of 2 sts plus 2 for foundation ch. *Yo, insert hk into ch or st as indicated, yo, draw lp thr, yo, draw thr 2 lps *, sk 1 ch or st, rep from *to *into next st, yo, draw thr all 3 lps on hk.

Row 1: Ch 3 (counts as first dc), 1 dcCL1 inserting hk first into first st, ch 1, *dcCL1 inserting hk first into same st as prev dcCL1, ch 1, rep from *end 1 dc in top of tch. Turn.

Row 2: Ch 1 (counts as first sc), sk 1 st, *sc in next ch sp, ch 1, sk 1 st, rep from *end 1 sc in top of tch. Turn.

Double crochet cluster stitch 2 (dcCL2): Any number of sts plus 2 for foundation ch.

Row 1: Ch 3 (counts as first dc), sk first st, dc2tog in every st across to last st, end 1 dc in top of tch. Turn.

Row 2: Ch 1 (counts as first sc), sk first st, sc in each st across end 1 sc in top of tch. Turn.

Dc2tog: Yo, insert hk into st, pl yarn thr, yo and pl thr 2 lps, yo, insert hk into same st, pl yarn thr (4 lps on hk), yo and pl thr 2 lps, yo and pl thr 3 lps.

INSTRUCTIONS:

Row 1: (RS) With Color A, ch 114 loosely. Make Lqtr by first inserting hk into and pl up lps in 2nd, 3rd, 4th, 5th, and 6th ch from hk, then insert hk into 7th ch and complete for 2nd Lqtr. (First 6 ch count as first Lqtr.) Cont across row. FO. Turn. (108 sts.)

Row 2: With Color B, attach yarn with a sc and sc across row, placing last sc in top of tch. Turn.

Rows 3–4: Ch 1, sc across. FO. Turn.

Row 5: With Color A, ch 6 and Lqtr across, FO. Turn.

Rows 6–8: With Color C, rep Rows 2–4.

Continued on page 86

84

Continued from page 84

Row 9: With Color A, rep Row 5.

Rows 10–12: With Color B, rep Rows 2–4.

Row 13: With Color A, ch 3, work Row 1 of dcCL1 across, end 1 dc in last sc. Turn.

Row 14: Ch 1, work Row 2 of dcCL1 across, end sc in tch. Turn.

Row 15: Ch 3, work Row 1 of dcCL2 across, *placing first dcCL2 in ch-1 sp, next dcCL2 in sc, rep from *end 1 dc in tch. Turn.

Row 16: Ch 1, work Row 2 of dcCL2 across, end 1 sc in tch. Turn.

Rows 17–81: Rep Rows 13–16 seventeen times, then rep Row 1 of dcCL1. FO.

Row 82: With Color B, ch 1, sc in first sc, *sc in next ch-1 sp, sc in next sc, rep from *across. Turn.

Rows 83–84: Rep Rows 3–4.

Row 85: With Color A, rep Row 5.

Rows 86–88: With Color C, rep Rows 2–4.

Row 89: With Color A, rep Row 5.

Rows 90–92: With Color B, rep Rows 2–4.

Row 93: With Color A, rep Row 5.

Edging:

Note:

- *Have an even number of sts on each side of afghan.*

Rnd 1: With WS facing and Color C, join with sc in any st other than a corner and sc around, placing 3 sc in each corner st, join with a sl st to beg sc. Turn.

Rnd 2: Ch 1, sc in each sc around, placing 3 sc in each corner st, sl st to beg sc. Turn.

Rnd 3: Ch 1, sc in each sc around, placing 3 sc in each corner st, sl st to beg sc, FO. Turn.

Rnd 4: Join Color C with sl st next to corner st on any side, ch 3 and *work Row 1 of dcCL1 to last sc bef next corner st, dc, [dc, ch 3, dc] in corner st, dc in next st, rep from *around, end sl st in top of beg ch-3. Turn.

Rnd 5: Ch 1, sc in each st and each ch-1 sp around, put 4 sc in corner ch-3 sp, sl st in top of beg st. Turn.

Rnd 6: Ch 1, sk first st and [sl st, ch 1] in each sc around, sl st to beg st, FO. Work in loose ends.

Diagonal Weave Afghan

Diagonal Weave Afghan

DESIGNED BY DELMA MYERS

Finished size: 52" x 68"

This "woven" afghan consists of 48 basic squares crocheted in a basket-weave style. Four squares are turned, placed, and stitched together to form a diamond design. The diamond squares are then stitched together horizontally and vertically.

MATERIALS:

Yarn: worsted weight
- Color A—Glade (24 oz.)
- Color B—Frosty Green (16 oz.)
- Color C—Tan (16 oz.)
- Color D—Light Sage (16 oz.)

Crochet hook: size G

Additional supplies:
- Tapestry needle

SPECIFICS:

Gauges: 3½ sts=1"; square=8"

Basic stitches used: ch, dc, hdc, rsc, sl st

Notes:
- *Ch 3 at beg of a row counts as a dc.*
- *When starting or end yarn, leave 8" tail for sewing square tog.*

- *To sew square tog, place two squares edge to edge, with stripes matching.*
- *Using tails in matching colors.*
- *Sew st in each square alternately; matching rows.*

INSTRUCTIONS:

Square: (Make 48.)

Row 1: With Color A, ch 6, dc in 4th, 5th, and 6th ch from hk. Turn. (First segment.)

Row 2: Ch 6, dc in 4th, 5th, and 6th ch from hk. Sl st in top of ch 3 of first segment, ch 3, 3 dc over ch post. Turn. (2 segments.)

Row 3: Ch 6, dc in 4th, 5th, and 6th ch from hk, [sl st in top of ch 3, ch 3, 3 dc over ch post] twice. Turn. (3 segments.)

Row 4: Ch 6, dc in 4th, 5th, and 6th ch from hk [sl st in top of ch, ch 3, 3 dc over ch post] three times. Turn. (4 segments.)

Row 5: Ch 6, dc in 4th, 5th, and 6th ch from hk [sl st to top of ch, ch 3, 3 dc over ch post] four times, FO. Turn. (4 segments.)

Row 6: Attach Color D in top of last dc, ch 6; dc in 4th, 5th, and 6th

ch from hk [sl st to top of ch, ch 3, 3 dc over ch post] five times. Turn.

Row 7: Ch 6, dc in 4th, 5th, and 6th ch from hk [sl st to top of ch, ch 3, 3 dc over ch post] six times. Turn.

Row 8: Ch 6, dc in 4th, 5th, and 6th ch from hk [sl st to top of ch, ch 3, 3 dc over ch post] seven times. Turn.

Row 9: Ch 6, dc in 4th, 5th, and 6th ch from hk [sl st to top of ch, ch 3, 3 dc over ch post] eight times. Turn. FO.

Row 10: Attach Color C in top of last dc, ch 6, dc in 4th, 5th, and 6th ch from hk [sl st to top of ch, ch 3, 3 dc over ch post, sl st to top of ch] nine times. Turn.

Row 11: Ch 6, dc in 4th, 5th, and 6th ch from hk [sl st to top of ch, ch 3, 3 dc over ch post] ten times. Turn.

Row 12: (Dec row.) Sl st in 3 dc and ch 3, [ch 3, 3 dc over ch post] ten times, FO. Turn.

Row 13: Attach Color B to top of ch 3 of last segment made, [ch 3, 3 dc over ch post, sl st to top of ch] nine times. Turn. (9 segments.)

Row 14: Sl st in 3 dc and ch 3, [ch 3, 3 dc over ch post, sl st to top of ch] eight times. Turn.

Row 15: Sl st in 3 dc and ch 3, [ch 3, 3 dc over ch post, sl st to top of ch] seven times. FO. Turn.

Row 16: Attach Color A in top of ch 3 of last segment made, [ch 3, 3 dc over ch post, sl st to ch] six times. Turn.

Row 17: Sl st in 3 dc and ch 3, [ch 3, 3 dc over ch post, sl st to top of ch] five times. Turn.

Row 18: Sl st in 3 dc and ch 3, [ch 3, 3 dc over ch post, sl st to top of ch] four times. Turn.

Row 19: Sl st in 3 dc and ch 3, [ch 3, 3 dc over ch post, sl st to top of ch] three times. Turn.

Row 20: Sl st in 3 dc and ch 3, [ch 3, 3 dc over ch post, sl st to top of ch] twice. Turn.

Row 21: Sl st in 3 dc and ch 3, ch 3, 3 dc over ch, sl st to top of ch. Sew squares tog fol Diamond Assembly Diagram.

Border:

Row 1: Attach Color A to any corner sp, [3 sc in corner, sc to next corner with sc in each dc and 2 sc over ch post] four times, sl st to first st.

Row 2: Ch 2, [3 hdc in corner, hdc in each sc to next corner] three times, 3 hdc in corner sc, hdc in each sc to beg, sl st to first st. FO. Turn.

Row 3: Attach Color B to a corner [3 hdc in corner, hdc in each hdc to next corner] four times, sl st to first st. FO. Turn.

Row 4: Attach Color C to a corner [3 hdc in corner, hdc in each hdc to next corner] four times, sl st to first st. FO. Turn.

Row 5: Attach Color D to a corner [3 hdc in corner, hdc in each hdc to next corner] four times, sl st to first st. FO.

Row 6: Attach Color A to any corner. Rsc in each hdc around. FO.

Diamond Assembly Diagram

89

Granny Afghan

DESIGNED BY MARGRET WILLSON

Finished size: 43" x 63"

Small crocheted squares are completed first, then joined into six blocks of sixteen squares each (four squares long and four squares wide). The large squares are then added to the completed blocks.

MATERIALS:

Yarn: worsted weight
Color A—Black (32 oz.)
Color B—assorted (27 oz.)
Notes:
- *Rnds 1 and 2 of each square require 5 yds of scrap color.*
- *Rnd 4 of large square requires 7 yds.*
- *Rnd 6 of large square requires 11 yds.*

Crochet hook: size H

SPECIFICS:

Gauge: Rnds 1 and 2=2½" across.

Basic stitches used: ch, dc, sc

INSTRUCTIONS:

Small square: (Make 96.)
Rnd 1: With Color B, ch 4, sl st in first ch to form ring, ch 4 (counts as dc + ch 1) [dc in ring, ch 1] seven times, sl st in 3rd ch of beg ch 4. (8 sps.)

Rnd 2: Sl st in next sp, ch 3, 2 dc in same sp, 3 dc in each rem sp, sl st in 3rd ch of beg ch-3. FO. (eight 3-dc grps.)

Rnd 3 (joining rnd):
First small square: Join Color A with sc in any sp bet 3-dc grps (ch-3, sc) in same sp, *[ch 3, sc in next sp, ch 3] (sc, ch 3, sc) in next sp, from *twice more, rep bet [ ], end with sl st in beg sc. FO.

Small square joined on one side:
Join Color A with sc in any sp bet 3-dc grps, [ch 3, sc] in same sp, ch 3, sc in next sp, ch 3, [sc, ch 1, sc in corner of adjoining square, ch 1, sc] in next sp, ch 1, sc in next sp of adjoining square, ch 1, sc in next sp, ch 1, sc in next sp of adjoining square, ch 1, [sc, ch 1, sc in next corner of adjoining square, ch 1, sc] in next sp, ch 3, sc in next sp, ch 3, [sc, ch 3, sc] in next sp, ch 3, sc in next sp, ch 3, join beg sc. FO.

Small square joined on two sides:
Join Color A with sc in any sp bet 3-dc grps, [ch 3, sc] in same sp, ch 3, sc in next sp, ch 3, [sc, ch 1, sc in corner of adjoining square, ch 1, sc] in next sp, [ch 1, sc in next sp of adjoining square, ch 1, sc in next sp, ch 1, sc in next sp of adjoining

square. Ch 1, (sc, ch 1, sc in next corner of adjoining square, ch 1, sc) in next sp] twice, ch 3, sc in next sp, ch 3, end sl st to join in beg sc.

Large square: (Make 46.)
Rnds 1–2: Rep Rnds 1 and 2 of Small square.

Rnd 3: Join Color A with sc in any sp bet 3-dc grps (sc, ch 3, sc) in same sp, *[ch 3, sc in next sp, ch 3] (sc, ch 3, sc) in next sp, rep from *twice more, rep bet [ ], join with sl st in beg sc. FO.

Continued on page 92

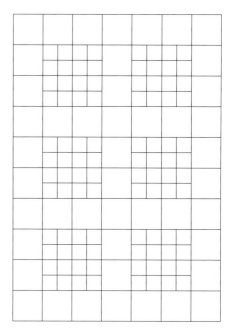

Granny Assembly Diagram

Continued from page 90

Rnd 4: Join Color B in any ch-3 corner sp, ch 3, (2 dc, ch 3, 3 dc) in same sp, *[3 dc in each of next 2 sps] (3 dc, ch 3, 3 dc) in next ch-3 corner sp, rep from *twice more, rep bet [ ], join with sl st in beg ch 3. FO.

Rnd 5: Join Color A with sc in any ch-3 corner sp, (ch 3, sc) in same sp, *[ch 3, (sc in next sp, ch 3) three times] (sc, ch 3, sc) in next corner sp, rep from *twice more, rep bet [ ], join with sl st in beg sc. FO.

Rnd 6: Join Color B in any ch-3 corner sp, ch 3, (2 dc, ch 3, 3 dc) in same sp, *[3 dc in each of next 4 sps] (3 dc, ch 3, 3 dc) in next ch-3 corner sp, rep from *twice more, rep bet [ ], join in beg ch 3. FO.

Joining Large squares:
Refer to Granny Assembly Diagram for placement of large squares. Where joined corners of two small squares meet the center side edge of a large square, ch-3 corners of small squares count as ch-3 sp and the joining point is sk. Where free corners of small square blks meet corners of large squares, joining is made in ch-3 corner sp. Where prev joined corners meet, the joining st counts as the corner and ch-3 corner sp are sk.

Joining Large square to corner of Small square block only: Join Color A with sc in any corner, (ch 3, sc) in same sp, ch 3 [(sc in next sp, ch 3) five times, (sc. ch 3, sc) in corner] twice, ch 3, (sc in next sp, ch 3) five times, (sc, ch 1, sc in free corner of Small square blk, ch 1, sc) in next corner sp, ch 3, (sc in next sp, ch 3) five times, join with sl st in beg sc. FO.

Joining Large square on two sides:
Join Color A with sc in any corner ch-3 sp, (ch 3, sc) in same sp, ch 3, (sc in next sp, ch 3) five times, [(sc, ch 1, sc in adjoining corner, ch 1, sc) in next corner sp, (ch 1, sc in next sp of adjoining square, ch 1, sc in next sp of current square) five times, ch 1, sc in next sp of adjoining square, ch 1] twice, (sc, ch 1, sc in adjoining corner, ch 1, sc) in next corner sp, ch 3, (sc in next sp of current square, ch 3) five times, join with sl st in beg sc, FO.

Joining Large square on three sides:
Join Color A with sc in any corner ch-3 sp, (ch 1, sc in adjoining corner, ch 1, sc) in same sp, [(ch 1, sc in next sp of adjoining square, ch 1, sc in next sp of current square) five times, ch 1, sc in next sp of adjoining square, ch 1, (sc, ch 1, sc in adjoining corner, ch 1, sc) in corner sp] three times. ch 3, (sc in next sp of current square, ch 3) five times, join in beg sc. FO.

Border: Join Color A in lower right ch-3 corner, ch 3, (2 dc, ch 3, 3 dc) in same sp, *(3 dc in each of next 6 sps, 3 dc in joining) nine times, 3 dc in each of next 6 sps, (3 dc, ch 3, 3 dc) in corner, (3 dc in each of next 6 sp, 3 dc in joining) six times, 3 dc in each of next 6 sps, (3 dc, ch 3, 3 dc) in next corner, rep from *once, end join with sl st in 3rd ch of beg ch-3. FO.

Crazy Squares Afghan

DESIGNED BY NANCY NEHRING

Finished size: 40" square

Solid double crochet is highlighted by contrasting variegated single crochet squares worked on the surface. Pattern works well in baby, sport, or worsted-weight yarns.

MATERIALS:

Yarn: light worsted weight
Color A—Amber (4 skeins)
Color B—Polo (3 skeins)
Crochet hook: size J

SPECIFICS:

Gauges: 12 dc=4"; 4½ rows=4"

Basic stitches used: bk lp, dc, sc, sl st

INSTRUCTIONS:

With Color A, ch 4. Sl st to join.

Rnd 1: Ch 3 (counts as first dc), 12 dc in ring. Sl st in bk lp only to join. Work all rem dc in bk lp only.

Rnd 2: Ch 3 (counts as first dc), *[dc in dc] twice, 5 dc in next dc (corner made) *rep around end with 5 dc in next dc. Sl st in bk lp to join.

Rem rnds: Ch 3 (counts as first dc), dc in each dc around except 5 dc in center dc of corner grp. Sl st in bk lp only to join. Work until piece is 38" square.

Last rnd: With Color B and working thr both lps of prev rnd, dc in each dc around except 5 dc in center dc of corner grp. Sl st to join. With Color B, attach yarn to free ft lp of any dc in Rnd 1. Working loosely, sc in each ft lp around. Sl st to join. Rep for all other rnds except last 2 rnds.

Mirror Image Afghan

DESIGNED BY RUTHIE MARKS

Finished size: 41" x 55" (excluding fringe)

This afghan consists of strips that are worked on both sides of the foundation chain so that Side 2 is a mirror image of Side 1. Every row begins and ends with an 8" tail to be incorporated later into the fringe. The first row of Side 2 is worked into the unused loops of the foundation row. Every strip is finished on both edges.

MATERIALS:

Yarn: 75% acrylic/25% wool
  Color A—Pale Aubergine
    (14 oz.)
  Color B—Aubergine (10½ oz.)
  Color C—Pale Sage Green
    (10½ oz.)
  Color D—Sage Green (10½ oz.)
Crochet hooks: sizes J, K
Additional supplies:
  Stitch markers
  Tapestry needle

SPECIFICS:

Gauges: Strip 1=2" x 55";
  Strips 2 & 4=5" x 55";
  Strip 3=3½" x 55"

Basic stitches used: sc, sl st
Special stitches used:
Picot single crochet (Psc): Insert hk, yo, draw lp thr, [yo, draw thr 1 lp] three times, yo, draw thr both lps on hk.
2-double crochet bobble (2-dcB): Yo, insert hk into next st, pl yarn thr, yo and pl thr 2 lps, yo, insert hk into same st, pl yarn thr, yo and pl thr 2 lps (3 lps on hk), yo and pl thr all lps.

INSTRUCTIONS:

Strip 1: (Make seven: two each of Colors A, C, and D, one of Color B.)
Note:
• *Sides 1 and 2 are the same.*
Row 1: (WS) With J hk, ch 168. Sc in 2nd ch from hk, *Psc in next ch, sc in next ch, rep from *to end, FO. Turn. (167 sts.)
Rows 2–3: Attach yarn with a sc and sc in each st across, FO, turn.
Row 4: Attach Color A with a sc, *ch 1, sk next st, sc in next st, rep from *across. FO.

Strip 2: (Make two.)
Note:
• *Sides 1 and 2 are the same.*
Row 1: (RS) With J hk and Color B, ch 168. Sc in 2nd ch from hk and each ch across. FO. Turn. (167 sts.)
Row 2: Attach Color D with a sc in the ft lp only, sc in ft lp only of each st across. FO. Turn.
Row 3: Attach Color B with sc in first st, in next st *dc in free lp of sc 2 rows below, inserting hk from bottom, sc in next st, rep from *across. FO. Turn.
Row 4: With Color C, rep Row 2.
Row 5: With Color B, rep Row 3.
Row 6: With Color B, rep Row 2.
Row 7: Attach Color A with a sc, *ch 1, sk next st, sc in next st, rep from *across. FO.

Strip 3, Side 1 (Make two.)
Row 1: (WS) With J hk and Color C, ch 168. Sc in 2nd ch from hk and each ch across. FO. Turn. (167 sts.)
Row 2: Attach Color C with a sc and sc in each st across. FO. Turn.
Row 3: Attach Color A with a sc, sc in next 5 sts, *ch 4, sc in next 6 sts, rep from *to last 5 sts, ch 4, sc in last 5 sts. FO. Turn.
Row 4: Attach Color D with a sc and sc in each st across, pl ch-4 lps toward you and working behind them. FO. Turn.
Row 5: Attach Color D with a sc and sc in each st across. FO. Turn.

Continued on page 96

Continued from page 94

Row 6: Attach Color A with a sc, *ch 1, sk next st, sc in next st, rep from *across. FO.

Strip 3, Side 2:

Row 1: (RS) Attach Color C with sc and sc in each st across. FO. Turn.

Row 2: Attach Color A with sc, sc in next 4 sts, *ch 4, sc in next 6 sts, rep from *to last 6 sts, ch 4, sc in last 6 sts. FO. Turn.

Rows 3–5: Rep Rows 4–6 of Side 1.

Strip 4 (Make two.)

Sides 1 and 2 are the same except for the color sequence. Color sequence for Side 1 is C, C, B, D, D, B, D, A. Color sequence for Side 2 is D, D, B, C, C, B, C, A.

Row 1: (RS) With J hk, ch 168. Sc in 2nd ch from hk and each ch across. FO. Turn. (167 sts.)

Row 2: Attach appropriate color with sc and sc in each st across. FO. Turn.

Row 3: Attach appropriate color with sc, *2dcB in next st, sc in next st, rep from *across. FO. Turn.

Rows 4–5: Rep Row 2.

Row 6: Attach appropriate color with sl st and sl st loosely in each st across. FO. Turn.

Row 7: Attach appropriate color with sc in top lp only of sl st, sc in top lp only of each sl st across. FO. Turn.

Row 8: Attach Color A with sc, *ch 1, sk next st, sc in next st, rep from *across. FO.

Joining strips:

Notes:
- *Use K hk to join all strips.*
- *To help with st counts, place stitch markers at regular intervals along sides of both pieces to be joined.*
- *Fol Joining Sequence Chart below for placement of strips.*

Placing RS tog, attach Color A with sl st and sl st loosely in each st across, going into the ft lp only of the strip closest to you and the bk lp only of other strip. FO.

Joining Sequence Chart:

Strip 1(Color D), 2,
   1(A), 3,
   1(C), 4
   (Color C side to the outside, Color D side to the inside),
   1(B), 4
   (Color D side to the inside, Color C side to the outside),
   1(C), 3,
   1(A), 2,
   1(D)

Fringe: (16" lengths.)

Using one strand of each color for each fringe, attach at even intervals across short ends of afghan. Using needle, thread ends left from making fabric thr the knots of the added fringe. Trim ends to even lengths.

Waves of Sunshine Afghan

Waves of Sunshine Afghan

DESIGNED BY RUTHIE MARKS

Finished size: 53" x 73"

Both the surface embellishment and the edging is worked with an N hook holding two strands of yarn together.

MATERIALS:

Yarn: 100% acrylic
Color A—Off-white (45½ oz.)
Color B—Jonquil (24½ oz.)
Color C—Fir (10½ oz.)
Crochet hooks: sizes H, N
Additional supplies:
Tapestry needle

SPECIFICS:

Gauge: With N hk and two strands of yarn, 4 sts and 4 rows sc=2"

Basic stitches used: dc, hdc, sc, sl st, tr

Special stitches used:

Picot: Sc, ch 4, sl st in sc just made.
Linked treble crochet (Ltr): Insert hk down thr upper of 2 horizontal lps rnd stem of prev st, yo and draw lp thr. Insert hk down thr lower horizontal lp of same st, yo and draw another lp thr. Treat these 2 lps as the wrappings which are required for an ordinary tr, insert hk in next st and complete st in normal way. To make first linked trc fol tch, insert hk into 2nd and then 4th chs from hk in order to pick up 2 preliminary lps. Complete st in normal way.

Color sequence:

Striped pattern:

Repeat sequence six times (72 rows): 4 rows A/A, 2 rows B/B, 4 rows A/A, 2 rows A/B.
Finish last 10 rows with 4 rows A/A, 2 rows B/B, 4 rows A/A.

INSTRUCTIONS:

With two strands of Color A and N hk, loosely ch 129.

Row 1: (RS) Sc in 2nd ch from hk and in next ch, hdc in next 2 chs, dc in next 2 chs, trc in next 4 chs, dc in next 2 chs, hdc in next 2 chs, *sc in next 4 chs, hdc in next 2 chs, dc in next 2 chs, trc in next 4 chs, dc in next 2 chs, hdc in next 2 chs; rep from *to last 2 chs, sc in last 2 chs. Turn. (128 sts.)

Rows 2 and 4: Ch 1, sc in each st across. Turn.

Row 3: Ch 1, sc in bk lp of each st across. Turn.

Row 5: Ch 4, Ltr in next st, dc in next 2 sts, hdc in next 2 sts, sc in next 4 sts, hdc in next 2 sts, dc in next 2 sts, *tr in next 4 sts, dc in next 2 sts, hdc in next 2 sts, sc in next 4 sts, hdc in next 2 sts, dc in next 2 sts; rep from *to last 2 sts, tr in next st, Ltr in last st. Turn.

Row 6: Rep Row 5 to last 2 sts, trc in next st, Ltr in top of tch. Turn.

Row 7: Ch 1, sc in each st across, end in tch. Turn.

Rows 8 and 10: Ch 1, sc in each st across. Turn.

Row 9: Ch 1, sc in bk lp of each st across. Turn.

Rows 11–12: Ch 1, sc in first 2 sts, hdc in next 2 sts, dc in next 2 sts, trc in next 4 sts, dc in next 2 sts, hdc in next 2 sts, *sc in next 4 sts, hdc in next 2 sts, dc in next 2 sts, trc in next 4 sts, dc in next 2 sts, hdc in next 2 sts; rep from *to last 2 sts, sc in last 2 sts. Turn.

Rows 13, 14, and 16: Ch 1, sc in each st across. Turn.

Row 15: Ch 1, sc in bk lp of each st across. Turn.

Rows 17–76: Rep Rows 5–16, five times.

Rows 77–81: Rep Rows 5–6 and then Rows 2–4.

Row 82: Rep Row 11. FO.

Surface embellishment:

Rows 3, 9, 27, 31, 57, 75, 86: With H hk and one strand of Color C, join with sl st in first free lp. Sc and sl st in same lp, [sl st, sc, sl st] in each free lp across. FO.

Edging:

Rnd 1: (RS) With H hk, in any st attach 1 strand of Color C with a sc, ch 1, [sc, ch 1] in each st on ends and evenly sp along sides, placing [sc, ch 1] three times in each corner st, sl st to beg sc. Turn.

Rnd 2: Ch 1, [sc, ch 1] in each sc around, placing [sc, ch 1] three times in middle sc of each corner grp, sl st to beg sc. Turn.

Rnd 3: Ch 3 (counts as 1 hdc and 1 ch), hdc in next sc, ch 1, [hdc, ch 1] in each sc around, placing [hdc, ch 1] three times in middle sc of each corner grp, sl st to 2nd ch of beg ch. Turn.

Rnd 4: Ch 1, sc in first st, ch 4, sl st in sc just made (picot made) ch 1, sk 1 st, *sc in next hdc, ch 1, sk 1 st, sc in next hdc, ch 4, sl st in sc just made, ch 1, sk 1 st, rep from *around, end with sl st in beg sc. FO. Adjust sts if necessary so a Picot ends up in middle hdc in each corner grp.

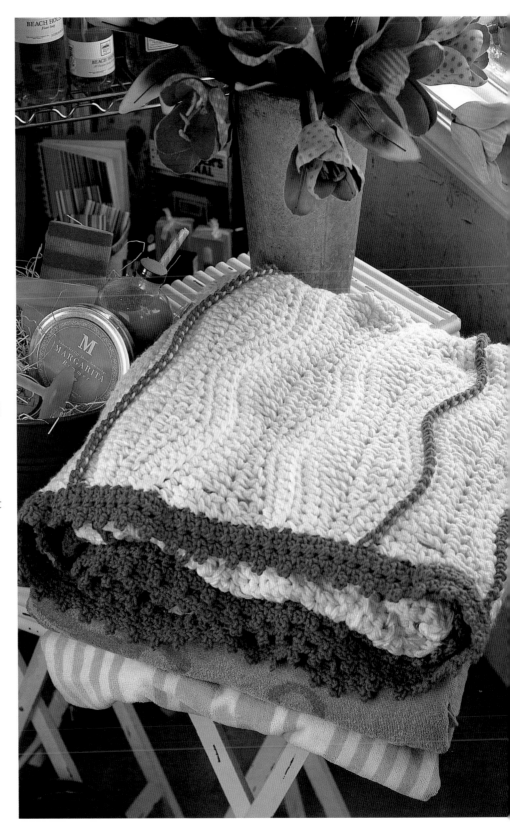

Easter Afghan

DESIGNED BY CAROL CARLILE

Finished size: 50" x 82"

Color is accentuated through the wide stripes. The popcorn stitch creates a pattern of diamonds throughout the stripes.

MATERIALS:

Yarn: Simply Soft
Color A—Off-white (26 oz.)
Color B—Orchid (26 oz.)
Color C—Sage (38 oz.)

SPECIFICS:

Gauges: 7 rows=2"; 10 sts=2"

Basic stitches used: ch, sc

Special stitch used:
Simple popcorn (pc)=ch 4

INSTRUCTIONS:

With Color A, ch 181.

Rows 1–5: Sc on 180 sts. Ch 1. Turn.

Row 6: (Start chg colors with this row.) 4 sc, pl up first half of 5th sc, *drop Color A, pick up Color C, finish 5th sc, work 19 sc and first half of 20th sc, drop Color C, pick up Color A, finish 20th sc, 4 sc and first half of 5th sc, drop Color A, pick up Color B and finish 5th sc, 19 sc and first half of 20th sc, drop Color B, pick up Color A and finish 20th sc, rep from *across row, end with 5 sc in Color A. (Three strips of Color B, four strips of Color C, eight strips of Color A.) Ch 1. Turn.

Row 7: Work even on 180 sc, chg colors as in Row 6. Ch 1. Turn.

Row 8: With Color A work 5 sc, with Color C work 20 sc, with Color A work 5 sc, with Color B work 20 sc, with Color A work 5 sc, with Color C work 20 sc, with Color A work 5 sc, with Color B work 20 dc, with Color A work 5 sc, with Color C work 20 sc, with Color A work 5 sc, with Color B work 20 sc, with Color A work 5 sc, with Color C work 20 sc, with Color A work 5 sc, ch 1, turn.

Row 9: Sc across row, chg colors in prev rows.

Row 10: With Color A, work 5 sc, with Color C work 8 sc, ch 4, 4 sc, ch 4, 8 sc, with Color A work 5 sc, with Color B, work 8 sc, ch 4, 8 sc, with Color A, work 5 sc, with Color C work 8 sc, ch 4, 4 sc, ch 4, 8 sc, with Color A work 5 sc, with Color B, work 8 sc, ch 4, 8 sc, with Color A, work 5 sc, with Color C work 8 sc, ch 4, 4 sc, ch 4, 8 sc, with Color A work 5 sc, with Color B, work 8 sc, ch 4, 8 sc, with Color A, work 5 sc, with Color C work 8 sc, ch 4, 4 sc, ch 4, 8 sc, with Color A work 5 sc, ch 1. Turn.

Row 11: Sc across row, chg colors in prev rows.

Row 12: With Color A work 5 sc, with Color C work 7 sc, ch 4, 6 sc, ch 4, 7 sc, with Color A work 5 sc, with Color B work 7 sc, ch 4, 7 sc, with Color A work 5 sc, with Color C work 7 sc, ch 4, 6 sc, ch 4, 7 sc, with Color A work 5 sc, with Color B work 7 sc, ch 4, 7 sc, with Color A work 5 sc, with Color C work 7 sc, ch 4, 6 sc, ch 4, 7 sc, with Color A work 5 sc, with Color B work 7 sc, ch 4, 7 sc, with Color A work 5 sc, with Color C work 7 sc, ch 4, 6 sc, ch 4, 7 sc, with Color A work 5 sc, ch 1. Turn.

Row 13: Sc across row, chg colors in prev rows.

Row 14: With Color A work 5 sc, with Color C work 6 sc, ch 4, 8 sc, ch 4, 6 sc, chg to Color A and work 5 sc, with Color B work 6 sc, ch 4, 8 sc, ch 4, 6 sc, with Color A work 5 sc, with Color C work 6 sc, ch 4, 8 sc, ch 4, 6 sc, with Color A work 5 sc, with Color B work 6 sc,

Continued on page 102

Continued from page 100

ch 4, 8 sc, ch 4, 6 sc, with Color A work 5 sc, with Color C work 6 sc, ch 4, 8 sc, ch 4, 6 sc, with Color A work 5 sc, with Color B work 6 sc, ch 4, 8 sc, ch 4, 6 sc, with Color A work 5 sc, with Color C work 6 sc, ch 4, 8 sc, ch 4, 6 sc, with Color A work 5 sc ch 1. Turn.

Row 15: Sc across row, chg colors as in prev rows.

Row 16: With Color A work 5 sc, with Color C work 5 sc, ch 4, 10 sc, ch 4, 5 sc, with Color A work 5 sc, with Color B work 5 sc, ch 4, 5 sc, ch 4, 5 sc, ch 4, 5 sc, with Color A work 5 sc, with Color C work 5 sc, ch 4, 10 sc, ch 4, 5 sc, with Color A work 5 sc, with Color B work 5 sc, ch 4, 5 sc, ch 4, 5 sc, ch 4, 5 sc, with Color A work 5 sc, with Color C work 5 sc, ch 4, 10 sc, ch 4, 5 sc, with Color A work 5 sc, with Color B work 5 sc, ch 4, 5 sc, ch 4, 5 sc, ch 4, 5 sc, with Color A work 5 sc, with Color C work 5 sc, ch 4, 10 sc, ch 4, 5 sc, with Color A work 5 sc ch 1. Turn.

Row 17: Sc across row, chg colors as in prev rows.

Row 18: With Color A work 5 sc, with Color C work 4 sc, ch 4, 12 sc, ch 4, 4 sc, with Color A work 5 sc, with Color B work 4 sc, ch 4, 5 sc, ch 4, 2 sc, ch 4, 5 sc, ch 4, 4 sc, with Color A work 5 sc, with Color C work 4 sc, ch 4, 12 sc, ch 4, 4 sc, with Color A work 5 sc, with Color B work 4 sc, ch 4, 5 sc,

ch 4, 2 sc, ch 4, 5 sc, ch 4, 4 sc, with Color A work 5 sc, with Color C work 4 sc, ch 4, 12 sc, ch 4, 4 sc, with Color A work 5 sc, with Color B, work 4 sc, ch 4, 5 sc, ch 4, 2 sc, ch 4, 5 sc, ch 4, 4 sc, with Color A work 5 sc, with Color C work 4 sc, ch 4, 12 sc, ch 4, 4 sc, with Color A work 5 sc, ch 1. Turn.

Row 19: Sc across row, chg colors as in prev rows.

Row 20: Work 5 sc in Color A, with Color C work 3 sc, ch 4, 14 sc, ch 4, 3 sc, with Color A work 5 sc, with Color B work 3 sc, ch 4, 5 sc, ch 4, 2 sc, ch 4, 2 sc, ch 4, 5 sc, ch 4, 3 sc, with Color A work 5 sc, with Color C work 3 sc, ch 4, 14 sc, ch 4, 3 sc, with Color A work 5 sc, with Color B work 3 sc, ch 4, 5 sc, ch 4, 2 sc, ch 4, 2 sc, ch 4, 5 sc, ch 4, 3 sc, with Color A work 5 sc, with Color C work 3 sc, ch 4, 14 sc, ch 4, 3 sc, with Color A work 5 sc, with Color B work 3 sc, ch 4, 5 sc, ch 4, 2 sc, ch 4, 2 sc, ch 4, 5 sc, ch 4, 3 sc, with Color A work 5 sc, with Color C work 3 sc, ch 4, 14 sc, ch 4, 3 sc, with Color A work 5 sc, ch 1. Turn.

Row 21: Sc across row, chg colors as in prev rows.

Rows 22–23: Rep Rows 18–19.
Rows 24–25: Rep Rows 16–17.
Rows 26–27: Rep Rows 14–15.
Rows 28–29: Rep Rows 12–13.
Rows 30–31: Rep Rows 10–11.
Row 32: With Color A work 5 sc,

with Color C work 9 sc, ch 4, 2 sc, ch 4, 9 sc, with Color A work 5 sc, with Color B work 9 sc, ch 4, 2 sc, ch 4, 9 sc, with Color A work 5 sc, with Color C work 9 sc, ch 4, 2 sc, ch 4, 9 sc, with Color A work 5 sc, with Color B work 9 sc, ch 4, 2 sc, ch 4, 9 sc, with Color A work 5 sc, with Color C work 9 sc, ch 4, 2 sc, ch 4, 9 sc, with Color A work 5 sc, with Color B work 9 sc, ch 4, 2 sc, ch 4, 9 sc, with Color A work 5 sc, Color C work 9 sc, ch 4, 2 sc, ch 4, 9 sc, with Color A work 5 sc, ch 1. Turn.

Row 33: Sc across row, chg colors as in prev rows.

Row 34: With Color A work 5 sc, with Color C work 10 sc, ch 4, 10 sc, with Color A work 5 sc, with Color C work 10 sc, ch 4, 10 sc, with Color A work 5 sc, with Color C work 10 sc, ch 4, 10 sc, with Color A work 5 sc, with Color C work 10 sc, ch 4, 10 sc, with Color A work 5 sc, with Color B work 10 sc, ch 4, 10 sc, with Color A work 5 sc, with Color C work 10 sc, ch 4, 10 sc; with Color A work 5 sc, with Color C work 10 sc, ch 4, 10 sc, with Color A work 5 sc, ch 1. Turn.

Row 35: Sc across row, chg colors as in prev rows.

Rows 36–37: Rep Rows 30–31.
Rows 38–39: Rep Rows 28–29.
Rows 40–43: Rep Rows 14–17.
Row 44: With Color A work 5 sc,

with Color C work 5 sc, ch 4, 5 sc, ch 4, 5 sc, ch 4, 5 sc, with Color A work 5 sc, with Color B work 5 sc, ch 4, 10 sc, ch 4, 5 sc, with Color A work 5 sc, with Color C work 5 sc, ch 4, 5 sc, ch 4, 5 sc, ch 4, 5 sc, with Color A work 5 sc, with Color B work 5 sc, ch 4, 10 sc, ch 4, 5 sc, with Color A work 5 sc, with Color C work 5 sc, ch 4, 5 sc, ch 4, 5 sc, ch 4, 5 sc, with Color A work 5 sc, with orchid work 5 sc, ch 4, 10 sc, ch 4, 5 sc, with Color A work 5 sc, Color C work 5 sc, ch 4, 5 sc, ch 4, 5 sc, ch 4, 5 sc, with Color A work 5 sc, ch 1. Turn.

Row 45: Sc across row, chg colors as in prev rows.

Row 46: With Color A work 5 sc, with Color C work 4 sc, ch 4, 5 sc, ch 4, 2 sc, ch 4, 5 sc, ch 4, 4 sc, with Color A work 5 sc, with Color B work 4 sc, ch 4, 12 sc, ch 4, 4 sc, with Color A work 5 sc, with Color C work 4 sc, ch 4, 5 sc, ch 4, 2 sc, ch 4, 5 sc, ch 4, 4 sc, with Color A work 5 sc, with Color B work 4 sc, ch 4, 12 sc, ch 4, 4 sc, with Color A work 5 sc, with Color C work 4 sc, ch 4, 5 sc, ch 4, 2 sc, ch 4, 5 sc, ch 4, 4 sc, with Color A work 5 sc, with Color B work 4 sc, ch 4, 12 sc, ch 4, 4 sc, with Color A work 5 sc, with Color C work 4 sc, ch 4, 5 sc, ch 4, 2 sc, ch 4, 5 sc, ch 4, 4 sc, with Color A work 5 sc, ch 1. Turn.

Row 47: Sc across row, chg colors as in prev rows.

Row 48: With Color A work 5 sc, with Color C work 3 sc, ch 4, 5 sc, ch 4, 2 sc, ch 4, 2 sc, ch 4, 5 sc, ch 4, 3 sc, with Color A work 5 sc, with Color B work 3 sc, ch 4, 14 sc, ch 4, 3 sc, with Color A work 5 sc, with Color C work 3 sc, ch 4, 5 sc, ch 4, 2 sc, ch 4, 2 sc, ch 4, 5 sc, ch 4, 3 sc, with Color A work 5 sc, with Color B work 3 sc, ch 4, 14 sc, ch 4, 3 sc, with Color A work 5 sc, with Color C work 3 sc, ch 4, 5 sc, ch 4, 2 sc, ch 4, 2 sc, ch 4, 5 sc, ch 4, 3 sc, with Color A work 5 sc, with Color B work 3 sc, ch 4, 14 sc, ch 4, 3 sc, with Color A work 5 sc, with Color C work 3 sc, ch 4, 5 sc, ch 4, 2 sc, ch 4, 2 sc, ch 4, 5 sc, ch 4, 3 sc, with Color A work 5 sc, ch 1. Turn.

Row 49: Sc across row, chg colors as in prev rows.

Row 50: With Color A work 5 sc, with Color C work 4 sc, ch 4, 5 sc, ch 4, 2 sc, ch 4, 5 sc, ch 4, 4 sc, with Color A work 5 sc, with Color B work 4 sc, ch 4, 5 sc, ch 4, 2 sc, ch 4, 5 sc, ch 4, 4 sc, with Color A work 5 sc, with Color C work 4 sc, ch 4, 5 sc, ch 4, 2 sc, ch 4, 5 sc, ch 4, 4 sc, with Color A work 5 sc, with Color B work 4 sc, ch 4, 5 sc, ch 4, 2 sc, ch 4, 5 sc, ch 4, 4 sc, with Color A work 5 sc, with Color C work 4 sc, ch 4, 5 sc, ch 4, 2 sc, ch 4, 5 sc, ch 4, 4 sc, with Color A work 5 sc, with Color B work 4 sc, ch 4, 5 sc, ch 4, 2 sc, ch 4, 5 sc, ch 4, 4 sc, with Color A work 5 sc, with Color C work 4 sc, ch 4, 5 sc, ch 4, 2 sc, ch 4, 5 sc, ch 4, 4 sc, with Color A work 5 sc, ch 1. Turn.

Row 51: Sc across row, chg colors as in prev rows.

Rows 52–63: Rep Rows 24–35.

Rows 64–345: Rep Rows 8–63 five times.

Rows 346–350: Work 5 rows in Color A. FO.

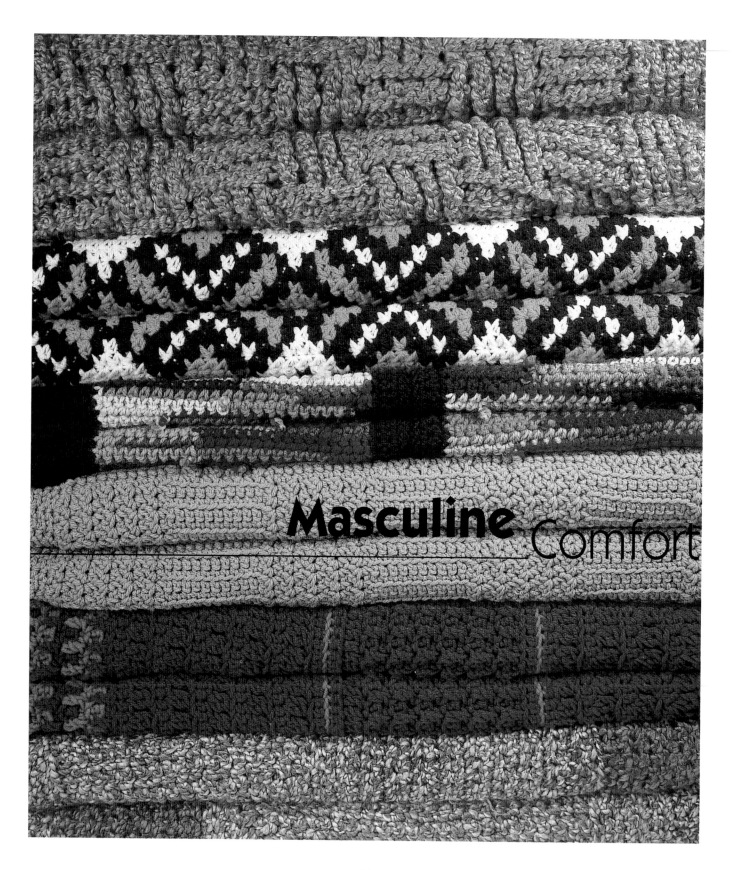

Masculine Comfort

Variegated Yarn Afghan

DESIGNED BY RUTHIE MARKS

Finished size: 42" square

The model used four compatible hues in two colorways—pink and green, picking up one color from each group to use as an accent color in the other group. The afghan is also an excellent way to use up leftover yarn. Another unique feature of this afghan is that the edging is done like the ribbing on a sweater.

MATERIALS:

Yarn: worsted weight,
75% acrylic/25% wool
Color A—Pale Pink (3½ oz.)
Color B—Light Pink (3½ oz.)
Color C—Medium Pink (3½ oz.)
Color D—Dark Pink (3½ oz.)
Color E—Pale Green (3½ oz.)
Color F—Light Green (3½ oz.)
Color G—Medium Green
     (3½ oz.)
Color H—Dark Green (3½ oz.)
Color J—Black (14 oz.)
Crochet hooks: sizes I, J
Additional supplies:
  Stitch markers
  Tape measure
  Tapestry needle

SPECIFICS:

Gauge: 7 rows and 6 sts=2"

Basic stitches used: ch, sc, sl st

Notes:
- *It takes approx 50 yds of tied-tog yarn to make an 8" square.*
- *Knots will appear at random on whichever side is easiest to manipulate. When finished, trim ends ¼" to ½" from knot.*
- *Color C becomes 5th (accent) color for green squares. Color G becomes 5th (accent) color for pink squares.*
- *Near ends of two strands held tog, tie an overhand knot and pl tight. Tie another overhand knot on top of first and pl tight again. Separate two strands and give each a tug, tightening knot for the 3rd time. Rep this process for each join.*

INSTRUCTIONS:

Cutting strands:
For one square, cut the fol lengths of A/B/C/D or E/F/G/H: six 40" strands each color and six 30" strands each color; and twelve 20" strands of 5th Color C or G. Lay out tape measure and loosely measure yarn. Do not pl tight or stretch in anyway.

Assembling strands: (Make sixteen balls of yarn, eight of each color.)

Method one (random approach):
Arrange yarn in two piles—one has forty-eight strands of pink (or green) that have been scrambled to be selected at random for length and color; the other pile has twelve strands of green (or pink) to be added at regular intervals.

Choose two strands at random from the large pile (two separate colors or two of the same color) and tie them tog. Choose another strand and tie it to the 2nd strand. Choose another strand and tie it to the 3rd strand. Now attach a 20" accent strand from the small pile. Rep to the end, tying four of the pink (or green) strands followed by a green (or pink) strand. Wind yarn into a loose ball.

Method two (orderly approach):
For a pink square, make separate piles of each color and each length. Tie a 40" length of Color A to a 40" length of Color B to a 40" length of Color C to a 40" length of Color D to a 20" length of Color G to a 30" length of Color A to a 30" length of Color B to a 30" length of Color C to a 30" length of Color D to a 20" length of Color G; rep to the end. Wind yarn into a loose ball. Use same method with green yarns.

Strips: (Make four.)

Row 1: With pink ball of yarn and J hk, ch 25. Sc in 2nd ch from hk and each ch across. Turn. (24 sc)

Row 2: Ch 1, sc in each sc across. Turn.

Rows 3–28: Rep Row 2. FO. Turn.

Row 29: Attach Color J with a sc and sc across. Turn.

Rows 30–34: Rep Row 2, FO. Turn.

Row 35: Attach green ball of yarn with a sc and sc across. Turn.

Rows 36–62: Rep Row 2. FO. Turn.

Rows 63–68: With Color J, rep Rows 29–34.

Rows 69–96: With a pink ball, rep Rows 35–62.

Rows 97–102: With Color J , rep Rows 29–34.

Rows 103–130: With a green ball, rep Rows 35–62. FO.

Edging:

Two strips (A and D) are for outside placement, two (B and C) are for inside placement. Add sc with Color J on inside long edges only of outside strips A and D; add sts with Color J to both long edges of strips B and C.

Row 1: (RS) With I hk, attach Color J in end of first sc on long edge of the strip. Sc in the end of each sc row. Turn. (130 sts.)

Row 2: Ch 1, sc in each sc across. Turn.

Row 3: Ch 1, sc in each sc across. FO.

Assembling strips:

With RS facing, place long inside edge of Strip A against long edge of Strip B. Place st markers at regular intervals along edges of both strips to help with st counting. With I hk join Color J in first sc with a sl st and sl st in each sc across, going into ft lp only of strip closest to you and into bk lp only of other strip. FO. Follow same procedure with Strips B and C and with Strips C and D. The outside edges of Strips A and D will have no sts at this point.

Edging:

Rnd 1: With I hk, attach Color J in any sc with a sc and sc around entire afghan, placing 3 sc in each corner st and one sc in the ends of each row along sides, end with an even number of sts bet each corner st. Sl st to beg sc. Turn.

Rnd 2: Ch 7, sc in 2nd ch from hk and in next 5 ch, sl st in next 2 sts on edge of afghan, ch 1, sc in bk lp only of next 6 sc on edge, turn, ch 1, sc in bk lp only of next 6 sc, sl st in next 2 sts on edge of afghan, rep from *around. Sl st last row to first row, going thr both lps of the last row and unused chs of the first row, FO.

On Rnd 2, work 5-corner sts as fol:

1: Sl st.

2: Sl st, ch 1, 6 sc blk, ch 1, 6 sc blk, sl st, ch 1, 6 sc blk, ch 1, 6 sc blk.

3: Sl st, ch 1, 6 sc blk, ch 1, 6 sc blk.

4: Sl st, ch 1, 6 sc blk, ch 1, 6 sc blk, sl st, ch 1, 6 sc blk, ch 1, 6 sc blk.

5: Sl st.

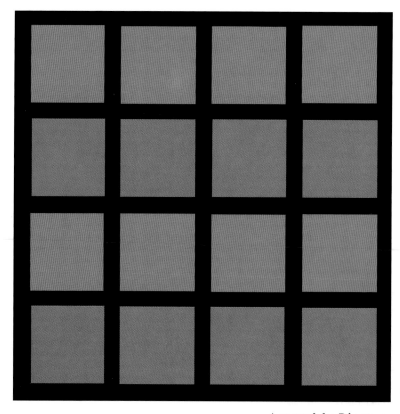

Assembly Diagram

Variegated Yarn Afghan

Basket-weave Afghan

DESIGNED BY MARTY MILLER

Finished size: 48" x 60"

The pattern used in the afghan shown is stretchy, and the gauge wasn't exact. However, if you crochet much tighter or looser, your yarn requirements will change.

MATERIALS:

Yarn: 98% acrylic/2% polyester, homespun
Royal Blue (42 oz.)
Crochet hook: size N

SPECIFICS:

Gauge: 6 post dc=approx 4"
5 patt rows=approx 4"

Basic stitches used: ch, dc, hdc

Special stitches used:

Front post double crochet (FPdc): Start dc around post of the st in row below, going from front to bk and around to front again. Finish dc as usual.

Back post double crochet (BPdc): Start dc around post of st in row below, going from bk to front and around to bk again. Finish dc as usual.

Patt st: *4 FPdc, 4 BPdc. Rep from *.

Notes:
- *The first ch 2 in each row and the last hdc in each row are not part of the patt sts.*
- *They do not count as FPdc.*

INSTRUCTIONS:

Ch 76 loosely.

Row 1: Dc in 4th ch from hk and in each ch across. Ch 2. Turn. (74 dc, including the first ch-3.) Rep patt nine times.

Row 2: Sk last dc in prev row. *Fpdc in next 4 dc. Bpdc in next 4 dc. Rep from *across. At end, hdc bet last BPdc made and ch 3 of prev row. Ch 2. Turn.

Row 3: Sk last st of prev row. *FPdc in next 4 sts. Bpdc in next 4 sts. Rep from *across. At end, hdc bet last BPdc made and ch 2 of prev row. Ch 2. Turn.

Row 4: Rep Row 3.

Row 5: Sk last st of prev row. *Bpdc in next 4 sts. Fpdc in next 4 sts. Rep from *across. At end, hdc bet last st made and ch 2 of prev row. Ch 2. Turn.

Rows 6–8: Rep Row 5.

Rows 9–12: Rep Row 3.

Rows 13–76: Rep Rows 5–12, for a total of 9 reps. FO. Weave in ends.

Basket-weave Blanket

DESIGNED BY AMY BREWER

Finished size: 42" x 58"

This one-piece blanket has a texture and a patchwork effect that is achieved using only single crochet and chains. Alternating the placement and number of stitches creates horizontal and vertical lines in the work, giving the illusion of woven bands.

MATERIALS:

Yarn: 100% acrylic worsted weight Warm Brown (38½ oz.)

Crochet hook: size H

Additional supplies:
Yarn needle

SPECIFICS:

Gauges: 4 sc=1"; 10 sc rows=3"

Basic stitches used: bk lp, ch, sc, sl st

INSTRUCTIONS:

Multiple of 20 + 10. Ch 130.

Row 1: [sc, ch 2, sc] in 2nd ch from hk, [sk next ch, (sc, ch 2, sc) in next ch] four times, *sc in next 10 ch, [sk next ch, (sc, ch 2, sc) in next ch] five times, rep from *across.

Rows 2–9: Ch 1, turn, [sc, ch 2, sc] in next 5 ch 2 sps, sk next st, *sc in ft lps of next 10 sts, [sc, ch 2, sc] in next 5 ch 2 sps, rep from *across.

Row 10: Ch 1, turn, 2 sc in next 5 ch 2 sps, *sk next st, sc in ft lps of next 10 sts, sk next st, 2 sc in next 5 ch 2 sps, rep from *across.

Row 11: Ch 1, turn, sc in ft lps of first 10 sts, *[(sc, ch 2, sc) in next st, sk next st] five times, sc in ft lps of next 10 sts, rep from *across.

Rows 12–19: Ch 1, turn, sc in ft lps of first 10 sts, *[sc, ch 2, sc] in next 5 ch 2 sps, sk next st, sc in ft lp of next 10 sts, rep from *across.

Row 20: Ch 1, turn, sc in ft lps of first 10 sts, *sk next st, 2 sc in next 5 ch 2 sps, sk next st, sc in ft lps of next 10 sts, rep from *across.

Row 21: Ch 1, turn, sk first st, [sc, ch 2, sc] in next st, [sk next st, (sc, ch 2 sc) in next ch] four times, *sc in ft lps of next 10 sts, [sk next st, (sc, ch 2, sc) in next ch] five times, rep from *across. Rep Rows 2–21 seven more times, then rep Rows 2–10 once more. Do not FO.

Edging:

Row 1: Ch 1, Do not turn, 3 sc in corner st, working down side, 1 sc in end of each row, 3 sc in each corner, 1 sc in top of each st, around. Sl st in first sc to join.

Row 2: Ch 1, sc in same st, *3 sc in corner st, sc in next st, sc alternating bk lp and ft lp down side, sc in last st bef corner, 3 sc in corner, sc in next st, sc alternating bk lp and ft lp across bottom, sc in last st bef corner, rep from *around. Sl st in first sc to join.

Row 3: Ch 1, sc in same st, sc in next st, *3 sc in corner, sc in next 2 sts, sc alternating bk lp and ft lp across, sc thr both lps of last 2 sts bef corner, rep from *around. Sl st in first sc to join.

Row 4: Ch 1, sc in same st, sc in next 2 sts, *3 sc in corner, sc in both lps of next 3 sts, sc alternating bk lp and ft lp across, sc in both lps of last 3 sts bef corner, rep from *around. Sl st in first sc to join. FO by weaving in loose ends with yarn needle.

Plum Pizzazz Afghan

DESIGNED BY RUTHIE MARKS

Finished size: 52" x 57"

By alternating the pattern and using contrasting colors to bind the panels, an interesting character and look is created.

MATERIALS:

Yarn: 100% acrylic
Color A—Dark Plum (32 oz.)
Color B—Teal (16 oz.)
Crochet hooks: sizes I & J
Additional supplies:
Tapestry needle

SPECIFICS:

Gauge: 7 dcCL=4"
Row Pattern: dcCL, sc, dc, sc, dcCL, sc, dcCL, sc, dcCL, sc=4"

Basic stitches used: dc, sc

Special stitch used:

Double crochet cluster (dcCL):
Yo, insert hk into st, pl yarn thr, yo and pl thr 2 lps; yo, insert hk into same st, pl yarn thr (4 lps on hk), yo and pl thr 2 lps, yo and pl thr 3 lps.

INSTRUCTIONS:

Note:

- *When making a dc in sts 2 rows below, insert hk from the bottom pointing up. Turn at the end of every row.*

Row 1: With J hk and Color A, ch 181. Dc in 4th ch and each ch across. Turn. (179 sts.)

Row 2: Ch 1, sc in ft lp only of each dc, end last st in ch 3. Turn.

Row 3: With Color B, ch 1, sc in bk lp only of first sc, *dc in free lp of st 2 rows below, sc in bk lp only of next dc, rep from *across. Turn.

Row 4: Ch 1, sc in ft lp only of each st, end last st in tch. Turn.

Rows 5–14: Rep Rows 3–4, fol the 2-row color sequence: A, B, A, B, A. Turn.

Row 15: With Color A, ch 2, sk first st, working under both lps dcCL in next st, *ch 1, sk one st, dcCL in next st, rep from *to last st, hdc in last st. Turn.

Row 16: Ch 1, sc in ft lp only of each st and ch across. Turn.

Rows 17–24: Rep Rows 15–16 four times.

Row 25: With Color B, join with a sl st, ch 1 and sl st loosely in both lps of each st across. Turn.

Row 26: With Color A, join with a sc and sc in top lp of each sl st across, end in first sl st. Turn.

Row 27: Ch 3, sk first st, dc thr both lps of each st across. Turn.

Row 28: Ch 1, sc in ft lp only of each st across. Turn.

Rows 29–40: With Color A, rep Rows 3-4 six times.

Rows 41–42: Rep Rows 25–26.

Rows 43–52: Rep Rows 15–16 five times.

Rows 53–54: Rep Rows 27–28.

Rows 55–66: Rep Rows 3–4 six times, fol the 2-row color sequence: B, A, B, A, B, A.

Rows 67–76: Rep Rows 15–16 five times.

Rows 77–78: Rep Rows 25–26.

Rows 79–80: Rep Rows 27–28.

Rows 81–92: With Color A, rep Rows 3–4 six times.

Rows 93–94: Rep Rows 25–26.

Rows 95–104: Rep Rows 15–16 five times.

Rows 105–106: Rep Rows 27–28.

Rows 107–118: Rep Rows 3–4 six times, fol the 2-row color sequence: B, A, B, A, B, A.

Edging:

Rnd 1: (RS) With I hk and Color A, join with a sc in any corner and sc around, placing 3 sc in each corner, sl st in bk lp of first sc. Do not turn.

Rnd 2: Ch 1, sc in bk lp only of each sc around, placing 3 sc in each corner, sl st to bk lp of first sc. FO Color A, do not turn.

Rnd 3: With Color B *[sc in bk lp, 3 sc in both lps, sc in bk lp] in corner sts, dc in free lp of st 2 rows below, sc in bk lp, dc in free lp of st 2 rows below to next corner grp, rep from *at each corner, sl st to beg st. FO. Work in loose ends.

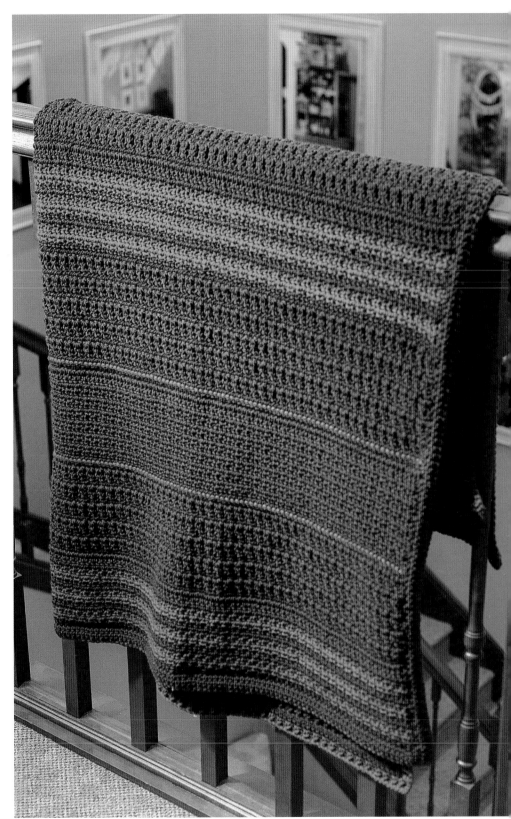

Southwest Jewel Afghan

DESIGNED BY DONNA J. BARRANTI

Finished size: 50" x 63"

A bold design is made with a jeweled border surrounding the diamond pattern within one another.

MATERIALS:

Yarn: Sport weight, 3-ply:
- Color A—Black (30 oz.)
- Color B—Pale Rose (10 oz.)
- Color C—Teal (20 oz.)
- Color D—White (10 oz.)

Crochet hook: size F

Additional supplies:
- Stitch marker

SPECIFICS:

Gauge: 9 star sts and 10 rows=4"

Basic stitches used: dc, sc

Special stitches used:

Beginning star stitch (beg star st): Yo, insert hk in 3rd ch from hk, yo and pl up a lp, yo, insert hk in eyelet of next star st, yo and pl up a lp, yo and draw thr all 5 lps on hk, ch 1 to close star st and form eyelet.

Star stitch (star st): Yo, insert hk in same eyelet as last leg of last star st made, yo and pl up a lp, yo, insert hk in eyelet of next star st, yo and pl up a lp, yo and draw thr all 5 lps on hk, ch 1 to close star st and form eyelet.

Ending star stitch (end star st): Yo, insert hk in same eyelet as last leg of last star st made, yo and pl up a lp, yo, insert hk in sp bef turning ch, yo and pl up a lp, yo and draw thr all 5 lps on hk. With Color A, ch 229 loosely, place st marker in 3rd ch from hk for st placement.

INSTRUCTIONS:

Row 1: (RS) Yo, insert hk in 3rd ch from hk, yo and pl up a lp, yo, sk next ch, insert hk in next ch, yo and pl up a lp, yo and draw thr all 5 lps on hk, *ch 1 to close star st and form eyelet, yo, insert hk in same ch as last leg of star st just made, yo and pl up a lp, yo, sk next ch, insert hk in next ch, yo and pl up a lp, yo and draw thr all 5 lps on hk; rep from *across. (113 star sts.)

Notes:
- *To chg color at beg of a row, hk new yarn and draw thr lp on hk, forming first ch of beg ch-3.*
- *To chg color within a row, work star st indicated to within one step of completion (one lp on hk), hk new yarn, and draw thr lp on hk, forming ch-1 eyelet. Work over unused color, holding yarn with normal tension and keeping it to WS of work.*
- *First ch of turning ch on next row will serve as eyelet for end star st.*

Row 2: Ch 3, turn; work beg star st, work 1 star st chg to Color C in last st, work 2 star sts chg to Color B in last st, work 3 star sts chg to Color A in last st, work 1 star st chg to Color B in last st, work 3 star sts chg to Color C in last st, work 2 star sts chg to Color A in last st, work 3 star sts chg to Color C in last st, rep from *, work 2 star sts chg to Color B in last st, work 3 star sts chg to Color A in last st, work 1 star st chg to Color B in last st, work 3 star sts chg to Color C in last st, work 2 star sts chg to Color A in last st, work 1 star st, work end star st.

Row 3: Ch 1, chg to Color C. Ch 2, turn; work beg star st chg to Color A in last st, *work 2 star st chg to Color C in last st, work 2 star sts chg to Color B in last st, work 5 star sts chg to Color C in last st, work 2 star sts chg to Color A in last st, work 2 star sts chg to

Continued on page 116

Continued from page 114

Color C in last st, work 1 star st chg to Color A in last st; rep from *six times more, work 2 star st chg to Color C in last st, work 2 star sts chg to Color B in last st, work 5 star sts chg to Color C in last st, work 2 star sts chg to Color A in last st, work 2 star sts chg to Color C in last st, work end star st.

Row 4: Ch 3, turn; work beg star st, work 1 star st chg to Color A in last st, *work 2 star st chg to Color C in last st, work 2 star sts chg to Color B in last st, work 3 star sts chg to Color C in last st, work 2 star sts chg to Color A in last st, work 2 star sts chg to Color C in last st, work 3 star sts chg to Color A in last st; rep from *six times more, work 2 star sts chg to Color C in last st, work 2 star sts chg to Color B in last st, work 3 star sts chg to Color C in last st, work 2 star sts chg to Color A in last st, work 2 star sts chg to Color C in last st, work 1 star st, work end star st.

Row 5: Ch 1, chg to Color A. Ch 2, turn; work beg star st chg to Color C in last st, *work 2 star sts chg to Color A in last st, work 2 star st chg to Color C in last st, work 2 star sts chg to Color B in last st, work 1 star st chg to Color C in last st, work 2 star sts chg to Color A in last st, work 1 star st chg to Color C in last st; rep from *six times more, work 2 star sts chg to Color A in last st, work 2 star st chg to Color C in last st, work 2 star sts chg to Color B in

last st, work 1 star st chg to Color C in last st, work 2 star sts chg to Color A in last st, work 2 star sts chg to Color C, work 2 star sts chg to Color A, work end star st.

Row 6: Ch 3 turn; work beg star st, work 1 star st chg to Color C in last st, work 2 star sts chg to Color A in last st, work 2 star st chg to Color C in last st, work 3 star sts chg to Color A in last st, work 2 star st chg to Color C in last st, work 2 star sts chg to Color A in last st, work 3 star st chg to Color C in last st; rep from *six times more, work 2 star sts chg to Color A in last st, work 2 star st chg to Color C in last st, work 3 star sts chg to Color A in last st, work 2 star st chg to Color C in last st, work 2 star sts chg to Color A in last st, work 1 star st, work end star st.

Row 7: Ch 1, chg to Color D. Ch 2 turn; work beg star st chg to Color A in last st, *work 2 star st chg to Color C in last st, work 2 star sts chg to Color A in last st, work 2 star st chg to Color C in last st, work 1 star st chg to Color A in last st, work 2 star st chg to Color C in last st, work 2 star sts chg to Color A in last st, work 2 star st chg to Color D in last st; work 1 star st chg to Color A in last st, rep from *six times more, work 2 star st chg to Color C in last st, work 2 star sts chg to Color A in last st, work 2 star st chg to Color C in last st, work 1 star st chg to Color A in last st, work 2 star st chg to Color C in last st, work 2 star sts

chg to Color A in last st, work 2 star st chg to Color D in last st, work end star st.

Row 8: Ch 1, chg to Color A. Ch 2, turn; work beg star st chg to Color D in last st, *work 1 star st chg to Color A in last st, work 2 star sts chg to Color C in last st, work 2 star st chg to Color A in last st, work 3 star st chg to Color C in last st, work 2 star st chg to Color A in last st, work 2 star sts chg to Color D in last st, work 1 star st chg to Color A, work 1 star st chg to Color D in last st; rep from *six times more, work 1 star st chg to Color A in last st, work 2 star sts chg to Color C in last st, work 2 star st chg to Color A in last st, work 3 star st chg to Color C in last st, work 2 star st chg to Color A in last st, work 2 star sts chg to Color D in last st, work 1 star st chg to Color A in last st, work end star st.

Row 9: Ch 3, turn; work beg star st, work 1 star st chg to Color D in last st, work 1 star st chg to Color A in last st, work 2 star sts chg to Color C in last st, work 1 star st chg to Color A in last st, work 1 star st chg to Color D in last st, work 1 star st chg to Color A in last st, work 1 star st chg to Color C in last st, work 1 star st chg to Color A, work 2 star sts chg to Color D in last st; rep from *six times more, work 1 star st chg to Color A in last st, work 2 star sts chg to Color C in last st, work 1 star st chg to Color A in last st, work 1 star st chg to Color D in last st, work 1 star st chg to Color A in last st, work 1 star st chg to Color C in last st, work 1 star st chg to Color A, work 2 star sts chg to Color D in last st, work 1 star st chg to Color A in last st, work 1 star st, work end star st.

Row 10: Ch 1, chg to Color C. Ch 2, turn; work beg star st chg to Color A, work 2 star sts chg to White in last st, work 1 star st chg to Color A in last st, work 2 star sts chg to Color D in last st, work 3 star sts chg to Color A in last st, work 2 star sts chg to Color D in last st, work 1 star st chg to Color A in last st, work 2 star sts chg to Color C in last st, work 1 star st chg to Color A in last st; rep from *six times more, work 2 star sts chg to Color D in last st, work 1 star st chg to Color A in last st, work 2 star sts chg to Color D in last st, work 3 star sts chg to Color A in last st, work 2 star sts chg to Color D in last st, work 1 star st chg to Color A in last st, work 2 star sts chg to Color C in last st, work end star st.

Row 11: Ch 3, turn; work beg star st, work 1 star st chg to Color A, *work 3 star sts chg to Color D in last st, work 5 star sts chg to Color A in last st, work 3 star sts chg to Color C in last st, work 3 star sts chg to Color A in last st; rep from *six times more, work 3 star sts chg to Color D in last st, work 5 star sts chg to Color A in last st, work 3 star sts chg to Color C in last st, work 1 star st, work end star st.

Row 12: Ch 3, turn; work beg star st, work 2 star st chg to Color A, *work 1 star st chg to Color D in last st, work 3 star sts chg to Color A in last st, work 1 star st chg to Color D in last st, work 3 star sts chg to Color A in last st, work 1 star st chg to Color C in last st, work 5 star sts chg to Color A in last st; rep from *six times more, work 1 star st chg to Color D in last st, work 3 star sts chg to Color A in last st, work 1 star st chg to Color D in last st, work 3 star sts chg to Color A in last st, work 1 star st chg to Color C in last st, work 2 star sts, work end star st.

Rows 13–21: Rep Rows 11–3.

Rows 22–141: Rep Rows 2–21 six times.

Row 142: Rep Row 2. FO.

Edging:

Rnd 1: Beg at lower left, using Color A, work star sts evenly sp across end of rows (working in eyelets and ch-3 sp); 3 dc in corner, work star sts across top of afghan (working in eyelets); 3 dc in corner; work star sts evenly sp across end of rows (working in eyelets and ch-3 sp); work star st in last ch-3 space. Ch 3, turn.

Rnds 2–7: Cont to work star sts across all four sides, ch 3. Turn at end of each rnd. In each corner, yo, insert hk in same eyelet as last leg of last star st made, yo and pl up a lp, yo, insert hk in 2nd dc in corner, yo and pl up a lp, yo and draw thr all 5 lps on hk, ch 1 to close star st, work 3 dc in same dc st, yo, insert hk in same dc st, yo and pl up a lp, yo, insert hk in eyelet of next star st, yo and pl up a lp, yo and draw thr all 5 lps on hk. Ch 1 to close star st and form eyelet; work star st in last ch-3 sp; ch 3. Turn.

Picot Edging: *[Ch 3, sc in first ch] sc in next two eyelets *rep around afghan placing one picot at each corner. FO.

Magic Square Lap Robe

DESIGNED BY JOYCE RENEE WYATT

Finished size: 42" x 56" without edging

The inspiration for this robe came from a knitted patchwork sweater designed by Irene York of the Knitting Basket in Tahoe City, CA. The motifs are crocheted using single crochet stitches without sewing them together later. Each square is picked up from an adjacent square and connected to one another as you go, using slipped stitches and/or chains. The size of the basic square will determine how many squares are needed.

MATERIALS:

Yarn: homespun
　　Color A—New England
　　　　(5 skeins)
　　Color B—Romanesques
　　　　(5 skeins)
Crochet hook: size N

SPECIFICS:

Gauge: 2.75 sts = 1";
　　square=14" square;
　　3 square x 4 square:=12 squares

Basic stitches used: sc, sl st

Special stitch used:

Dec=sc2tog (sc 2 sts tog)
Note:
- *Make each square using a new skein.*

INSTRUCTIONS:

Square 1:

Ch 81.

Row 1: Sc in 2nd ch from hk and in each of the next 37 chs across, [sc2tog] twice; sc in rem 38 chs. Ch 1. Turn.

Row 2: Sc in next 37 sts, [sc2tog] twice; sc in rem 37 sts. Ch 1. Turn.

Row 3: Sc in next 36 sts, [sc2tog] twice; sc in rem 36 sts. Ch 1. Turn.

Row 4: Sc in next 35 sts, [sc2tog] twice; sc in rem 35 sts. Ch 1. Turn.

Row 5: Sc in next 34 sts, [sc2tog] twice; sc in rem 34 sts. Ch 1. Turn.

Row 6: Sc in next 33 sts, [sc2tog] twice; sc in rem 33 sts. Ch 1. Turn.

Row 7: Sc in next 32 sts [sc2tog] twice; sc in rem 32 sts. Ch 1. Turn.

Row 8: Sc in next 31 sts [sc2tog] twice; sc in rem 31 sts. Ch 1. Turn.

Row 9: Sc in next 30sts [sc2tog] twice; sc in rem 30 sts. Ch 1. Turn.

Row 10: Sc in next 29 sts [sc2tog] twice; sc in rem 29 sts. Ch 1. Turn.

Row 11: Sc in next 28 sts [sc2tog] twice; sc in rem 28 sts. Ch 1. Turn.

Row 12: Sc in next 27sts [sc2tog] twice; sc in rem 27 sts. Ch 1. Turn.

Row 13: Sc in next 26 sts [sc2tog] twice; sc in rem 26 sts. Ch 1. Turn.

Row 14: Sc in next 25 sts [sc2tog] twice; sc in rem 25 sts. Ch 1. Turn.

Row 15: Sc in next 24sts [sc2tog] twice; sc in rem 24 sts. Ch 1. Turn.

Row 16: Sc in next 23 sts [sc2tog] twice; sc in rem 23 sts. Ch 1. Turn.

Row 17: Sc in next 22 sts [sc2tog] twice; sc in rem 22 sts. Ch 1. Turn.

Row 18: Sc in next 21 sts [sc2tog] twice; sc in rem 21 sts. Ch 1. Turn.

Row 19: Sc in next 20 sts [sc2tog] twice; sc in rem 20 sts. Ch 1. Turn.

Row 20: Sc in next 19 sts [sc2tog] twice; sc in rem 19 sts. Ch 1. Turn.

Rows 21–37: Cont dec in establish patt until 6 sts rem. Ch 1. Turn.

Row 38: Sc in next st, [sc2tog] twice; sc in rem st. Ch 1. Turn.

Row 39: [Sc2tog] twice. Ch 1. Turn.

Row 40: [SC 2tog] once. FO. Turn square so FO tail is positioned at upper right-hand corner.

Continued on page 120

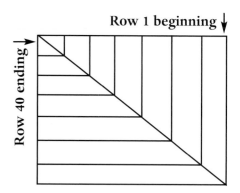

118

Square 2:

Using Color B Ch 40; sl st 40 sts very loosely across top of Square 1, Ch 1. Turn. (Ttl of 81 chs/sl sts.) With WS of work facing you, work 1 sc in each of top lps of the 38 sl sts; sc2tog.

Note:

- *When working sc, do not work into selvedge edge of prev square. This edge will give squares a decorative cord-like look on the WS.*

At this point, you now have 40 chs rem. With WS of foundation ch facing you, and working in top lps only: sc2tog, sc in the rem 38 chs. Beg with Row 2 to complete Square 2. You have connected Square 2 to Square 1 without sewing.

Note:

- *Each additional square is joined with foundation chs and/or sl st. Always work Row 1 into the top lps only of each sl st, and also into the top lps on the WS of the foundation ch.*

Work sc sts in Rows 2-40 into both lps.

Square 1   **Chain 40 →**

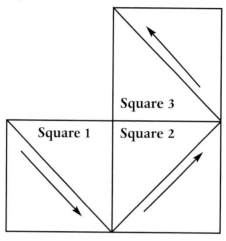

Sl st 40 sts across top if Square 1; plus 1 extra ch. Total of 81 chs/sl sts.

Square 3:

Using first small ball of Color A, Ch 40; sl st 40 sts across along left side of Square 4. Ch 1. Turn. (Total of 81 chs/sl sts.) When Color A is finished, attach Color B until finished, then attach Color A. Connect Square 3 using Color A same as you connected Square 2 to Square 1. The FO tail from Square 2 should be positioned at upper right-hand corner.

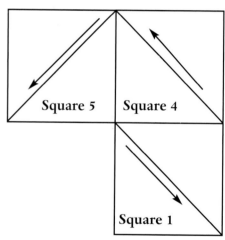

Drawing above shows Squares 1–3 completed. Arrows show direction of the diagonal line and the position of the FO tail.

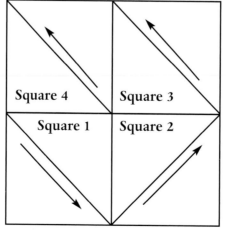

Square 4:

Using Color B; work 40 sl sts along left side edge of Square 3, and work 40 sl sts across the top of Square 1. Ch 1. Turn. You have completed four squares. You should have 2 small balls of left over yarns from Color A and Color B. This yarn is used to make Square 5.

Square 5:

Using first small ball of Color A, Ch 40; sl st 40 sts across along left side of Square 4. Ch 1. Turn. (Total of 81 chs/sl sts.) When Color A is finished, attach Color B until finished, then attach Color A.

Square 6:

Using new skein of Color B, sl st 40 sts across bottom of Square 5; sl st 40 sts along left side of Squares 1. Ch 1. Turn.

120

Square 7:

Using Color A, Ch 40; sl st 40 sts across the bottom of Square 6. Ch 1. Turn.

Note:
• *Squares 5, 8, & 10 are made using leftover yarns.*

Connect Squares:

Connect Squares 10-12 to Squares 3-5.

Square 5, start with Color A, Color B, and finish with Color A. Square 8, start with Color B, Color A and finish with Color B. Square 10, start with Color B and finish with Color A. Do not FO aft completing Square 12. This same yarn is used for edging.

Edging:

Rnd 1: Sl st 40 sts for each square; make a Ch 1 for each the three corners, end with Ch 1 (this is the 4th corner) and join with sl st to first sl st make on Square 12. Ch 1. Do not turn.

Rnd 2: Work sc into top half of each sl st; and work 3 sc in ch 1 sp at each corner. Join with sl st to first sc. Ch 1, do not turn.

Rnds 3–4: Work sc into first st and in each sc around, working 3 scs into 2nd st of each 3 sc grp at each corner. FO. Weave in loose ends.

Square 12	Square 11	Square 10
Square 5	Square 4	Square 3
Square 6	Square 1	Square 2
Square 7	Square 8	Square 9

The Designers

Donna J. Barranti

"At the age of eleven, my grandmother taught me how to crochet pineapple sachets. I soon found great pleasure in crocheting afghans. I love to spend my leisure time creating colorful crochet patterns. I also enjoy knitting, sewing, and quilting."

Donna is married with two daughters and four grandchildren. She is employed as the Federal Documents Specialist for the Olin Library at Rollins College in Winter Park, FL.

She has published patterns in *Crochet World*, October 1996; *Crochet With Heart*, February 2000; *Warm & Cuddly, Afghans for All Seasons: Book 3*, 2002; *Cinnamon Dreams*, Leisure Arts, Inc., scheduled for future publication.

Amy Brewer

Amy learned to crochet at the age of nine at the knee of her mother. A year later, her fifth-grade teacher, Mrs. Finley, encouraged her love of crochet by allowing her to stay in during recess and helping her with crochet. Her paternal grandmother further encouraged her by purchasing many of the toys she would crochet.

Amy began designing in 1999 while stationed overseas with her Air Force husband Clinton. English written patterns were scarce, so she set about building up her own pattern library. She has had patterns published in *Crochet World, Crochet!,* and *Crochet Fantasy*.

Crochet has been a big help to Amy in her own Air Force career as a parachute rigger. Through crochet, she had already learned the skill of removing knots without damaging fibers, a skill highly sought after when untangling suspension lines.

Carol Carlile

"When I was about eight years old, my cousin tried to teach me to crochet, with little success. Then when I had my children, I got a book and taught myself to crochet and the rest is history. Needless to say, my children wore some of my designs. Now my grandchildren are wearing my designs."

Carol began crocheting professionally in 1995 and has sold to several craft companies, including: Annie's Attic, The Needlecraft Shop, House of White Birches, Crochet Fantasy, Herrschner's, Coats & Clark, and Kooler Design Studios. She was able to quit her secretarial job four years ago and go fulltime with her crochet business.

Joan A. Davis

Joan teaches crochet courses in the Palm Beach County School Adult Education Program. She has taught at Miami-Dade Community College, Clayton State College and University, as well as seminars and workshops. She has started a children's program at the City of West Palm Beach Library and another with Coral Reef Montessori Charter School.

Joan is a freelance writer for *Crochet Fantasy Magazine*. Her work was showcased at the 2001 and 2002 Crochet Guild of America Conferences.   She was one of the founding members of the Crochet Guild of America in 1994 and taught crochet classes at its first conference at DePaul University.

Joan is certified through the Craft Yarn Council of America and Crochet Design of England. She is an active member of the Crochet Guild of America as Industry Liaison, was the 2002 Local Conference co-Chairperson of the Chain Link Crochet Conference held in Palm Beach Gardens, and founded the Tropical Crochet Guild of the Palm Beaches in December 2000. In July 2003, Joan was a featured instructor at the Crochet Guild of America Conference.

She is currently a member of The National Needlework Association and the Crochet Guild of America. Joan has more than 30 years experience. Her most recent venture is developing a company of her own, Designs 4 Crochet LLC.

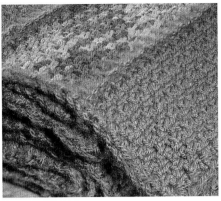

Roberta J. Gardner

"My mom's favorite pastime was crochet, but guess who was too busy with school, career, and family to learn the art.

After I retired and my mom passed away, I inherited hooks, needles, threads, and many small balls of colorful yarns. What to do with so many of her treasures? Why, design teddy bear sweaters, of course."

C. Yvette Holmes

Crocheting since the age of eight, Yvette enjoys the creative and artistic possibilities crochet provides. She shares her love of crochet by teaching others. She is an active member of the Alamo Metro Crochet Guild, the Knitters and Crocheters Guild of Austin, Texas and the Crochet Guild of America.

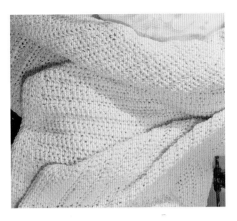

Carol Lykins

Carol has been crocheting since being taught at an early age by her grandmother. She works with her sister Janet Rehfeldt and Knitted Threads Designs as a contract crocheter and pattern editor. They have co-designed many projects over the years, and although Carol enjoys keeping in the background, she is quite a designer in her own right. Carol lives in Klamath Falls, OR, with her husband.

Ruthie Marks

Ruthie is a Southern California native who learned to crochet about seven years ago after an early retirement. She lives in Ojai, with her husband Roger and three cats that love to help unwind yarn skeins.

"I didn't learn to crochet earlier because I couldn't find a teacher who was left-handed. But when I came to Ojai I discovered a group of right-handed ladies who just sat me down and showed me how anyway!"

Marty Miller

Marty has been crocheting and creating her own patterns since she was a little girl. Using all kinds of yarns, she designs and makes afghans, sweaters and jackets, toys and puppets, scarves and shawls, tote bags, and more. She teaches crochet, designs for a yarn company, and also self-publishes her own patterns. When she's not crocheting, she is a group exercise instructor and personal trainer.

Delma Myers

Delma taught herself to crochet 45 years ago when given an unfinished granny square afghan. She is a CYCA certified instructor, has a crochet diploma from England, and is a charter member of both CGOA and Ididachain Crochet Guild of Alaska. Delma currently devotes her time to crochet design, and has a sweater published in *Today's Crochet—Sweaters* from the Crochet Guild of America.

Willena Nanton

Willena has been crocheting for about 27 years. She is the former president and a current member of the NYC Crochet Guild, Inc. She has been a Craft Yarn Council of America certified crochet instructor since 1995.
Willena currently teaches a beginner's crochet course for adults. She enjoys crocheting afghans, baby booties and sweaters, and adult wearables.

In 1994, she donated blankets to a homeless shelter. Since that time, she has worked with children in public middle schools to create and connect crocheted squares to make blankets for the children living in a homeless shelter. In 2003, she had a crochet hat design published in the book *Today's Crochet-Sweaters* from the Crochet Guild of America.

Nancy Nehring

Nancy is a nationally recognized author, teacher, and designer in the needle-arts field. She is the author of several books including *Beaded Embellishments.* Numerous needle-art magazines, including *Threads and PieceWork,* have carried her work. She has designed for DMC, Donna Karan, and Dynamic Resources Group, among others.

Nancy lectures and teaches locally, regionally, and nationally, including Embroiderers' Guild of America Seminar, Crochet Guild of America Chain Link, and Stitches.

Joy M. Prescott

Joy learned to crochet in the mid '70s while fishing off an island in Alaska, where she spent much of her life. Since 1980, Joy's patterns have been published in many magazines and several books. Now a resident of Washington state, Joy belongs to the Crochet Guild of Puget Sound, is a professional member of the Crochet Guild of America, and participates in an informal crochet group that meets weekly.

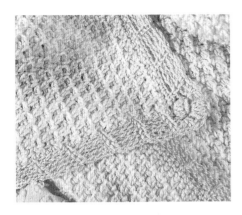

Janet Rehfeldt

Janet has been knitting and crocheting since the age of seven. She is the owner of Knitted Threads Designs, and an instructor, designer, and author. Her designs can be found in leading knitting and crochet publications. She authored *Crocheted Socks! 16-Fun-To-Stitch-Patterns* from Martingale Publications and *Toe Up Techniques For Hand Knit Socks* from Montat Publications. She does instruction on both local and national levels. Janet lives in Sun Prairie, WI, with her husband.

Kathleen Stuart

Kathleen learned to crochet when she was 10 years old and has been crocheting and designing crochet ever since. She's a professional member of the Crochet Guild of America and enjoys attending her local Chapter, South Bay Crochet. Kathleen's designs have appeared in publications from the Needlecraft Shop, House of White Birches, Leisure Arts, and All American Crafts. Kathleen lives in San Jose, CA, with her husband, Harold and their four children.

Margret Willson

Margret is a freelance designer whose work has appeared in various magazines and pattern collections. Experimenting with color, texture, and new techniques keeps her in love with the art of crochet. Margret is a professional member of the Crochet Guild of America (CGOA). She lives in Salt Lake City, Utah.

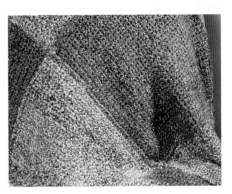

Joyce Renee Wyatt

Joyce says, "God has blessed me with the gifts of knitting and crochet"—gifts she enjoys sharing with others. This skillful knitter, crocheter, designer, and teacher has seen many of her designs and articles published in national magazines. Joyce teaches knitting/crochet classes at Joann's ETC Fabric Store in Torrance, CA. She has taught for local knitting/crochet guilds, Stitches Expos, TKGA, TNNA, and CQOA. She is a certified knitting/crochet instructor with the Craft Yarn Council of America.

Materials:

Aran Afghan (pg. 78):
Coats & Clark TLC Essentials Winter
  White

Baby, Baby Afghan (pg. 18):
Patons' Look At Me Baby Sport,
60% acrylic/40% nylon
  A—White #6351
  B—Lagoon #6361
  C—Lilac #6358
  D—Green Apple #6352
  E—Mid Blue # 6359
  F—Fun'n Games Variegated #6377

Baby Blocks Afghan (pg. 14):
Bernat Cottontots, 100% cotton
  A—Wonder White #90005
  B—Sweet Green #90230
  C—Sunshine #90615
  D—Pretty in Pink #90420
  E—Little Boy Blue #90128

Baby Car Seat Cover (pg. 20):
Lion Brand Homespun
  A—Deco #309
  B—Inca #357
  C—Cyprus #358

Basket-weave Afghan (pg. 108):
Lion Brand Homespun,
98% acrylic, 2% polyester
  Williamsburg #321

Basket-weave Blanket (pg. 110):
Coats & Clark Red Heart Classic, 100%
acrylic, worsted weight
  Warm Brown #336

Carnival Afghan (pg. 68):
  A—Bernat 4-ply acrylic Hot Pink
  B—Lion Brand Polar Spun Hot Pink
  C—Bernat Soft Boucle Strawberry
  D—Lion Brand Fun Fur Hot Pink
  E—Lion Brand Homespun Mardi Gras

Colorful Squares Afghan (pg. 82):
Red Heart, worsted weight
  A—Watercolor
  B—Light Plum
  C—Light Sage
  D—Frosty Green

Confetti Baby Afghan (pg. 24):
Red Heart TLC Baby, sport weight
  Naptime # 5964
  Powder Blue # 5881

Cool Cotton Throw (pg. 74):
Coats & Clark Aunt Lydia's Denim Quick
Crochet, 75% cotton/25% acrylic
  A—Milk #1002
  B—Linen #1021

Cozy Country Afghan (pg. 36):
Caron Simply Soft, 100% acrylic, worsted
weight
  A—Country Blue #9710
  B—Off White #9702

Crazy Squares Afghan (pg. 93):
Coats TLC, light worsted weight
  Amber
  Polo

Diagonal Weave Afghan (pg. 87):
Red Heart Fiesta and Supersaver,
worsted weight
  A—Glade
  B—Frosty Green
  C—Tan
  D—Light Sage

Emerald Isle Afghan (pg. 50):
Worsted weight yarn
  A—Variegated
  B—Contrasting

Fiesta Time Afghan (pg. 52):
Worsted weight yarn
  A—Off-white
  B—Red
  C—Green
  D—Yellow
  E—Blue
  F—Coral

Fish Afghan (pg. 65):
Coats & Clark Red Heart Kids
100% acrylic
  Periwinkle
  Yellow
  Red
  Lime

Floating on Air Afghan (pg. 17):
Red Heart Baby Clouds,
bulky bouclé weight
  Tutti-frutti #9351

Galaxy Afghan (pg. 42):
Red Heart sport weight
  Hunter Green
  Off White
  Yellow

Granny Afghan (pg. 90):
Worsted weight
  Black
  Assorted scrap colors

Growing Garden Afghan (pg. 54):
Red Heart Kid Colors
  Happy
  Lime
Red Heart Super Saver
  Coffee

Here's My Heart Afghan (pg. 46):
Red Heart Super Saver,
4-ply worsted weight
  Grey Heather #0400
  Burgundy #376
  Aran Fleck #4313
  Warm Brown #336
  Black #312

Lacy Lattice Afghan (pg. 76):
Worsted weight
  Off-white
Lion Brand
  Antique White #099

Light Plum Afghan (pg. 72):
Red Heart Super Saver, 100% acrylic,
  Light Plum #579

Linked Quads Afghan (pg. 84):
Red Heart Super Saver,
100% acrylic, worsted weight
  A—Monet #310
  B—Light Periwinkle #347
  C—Frosty Green #661

Loop-the-Loop Afghan (pg. 38):
Red Heart Soft, 100% acrylic
  A—Light Yellow Green #7675
  B—Dark Yellow Green #7672

Love Afghan (pg. 56):
Red Heart KIDS
100% acrylic, worsted weight
  Turquoise #2850
  Lime #2652
  Orange #2252
  Orchid #2360
  Yellow #2230
  Green #2677
  Blue #2845
  Pink #2734
  Red #2390

Magic Square Lap Robe (pg. 118):
Lion Brand Homespun
    A—New England
    B—Romanesques

Mirror Image Afghan (pg. 94):
Paton's Decor, 75% acrylic, 25% wool
    A—Pale Aubergine #1625
    B—Aubergine #1626
    C—Pale Sage Green #1635
    D—Sage Green #1636

Mosaic Ripple Afghan (pg. 12):
Baby yarn:
    Blue
    Pink
    White
    Yellow

Pink Square Baby Afghan (pg. 23):
Red Heart baby sport
    Pink

Plum Pizzazz Afghan (pg. 112):
Red Heart Super Saver, 100% acrylic
    A—Dark Plum #533
    B—Teal #388

Quick and Easy Afghan (pg. 31):
Lion Brand Homespun,
98% acrylic, 2% polyester
    Pacifica #317

Rainbow Blocks Afghan (pg. 62):
Worsted weight yarn, 100% acrylic
    A—Red
    B—Orange
    C—Yellow
    D—Green
    E—Blue
    F—Violet

Ruffle Baby Afghan (pg. 32):
Red Heart Soft Baby

Southwest Jewel Afghan (pg. 114):
Red Heart 3-ply sport weight
    Black
    Teal
    White
    Pale Rose

Take 'n Make Afghan (pg. 60):
Red Heart, worsted weight
    Amethyst
    Gemstone
Lion Brand Jiffy
    Forest Green

Variegated Yarn Afghan (pg. 105):
Plymouth Encore, knitting worsted
weight 75% acrylic, 25% wool
    A—Pale Pink #9408
    B—Light Pink #180
    C—Medium Pink #1607
    D—Dark Pink #999
    E—Pale Green #801
    F—Light Green #9401
    G—Medium Green #1604
    H—Dark Green #204
    I—Black #217

Waves of Sunshine Afghan (pg. 97):
Caron 100% acrylic
    Wintuk
    Off-white #3002
    Jonquil #3256
Sayelle:
    Fir #0426

Wedding Present Afghan (pg. 40):
Lion Brand Wool-Ease Chunky,
80% acrylic, 20% wool
    A—Bluebell #107
    B—Fisherman #099

Zigzag Baby Afghan (pg. 22):
Red Heart Baby sport pompadour
    Mint Green

Crochet hook conversion chart

United States	Size	Metric	Canada/U.K.
B	1	2.25	13
B	2	2.75	
D	3	3.25	10
E	4	3.50	9
F	5	4.00	
G	6	4.25	8
H	8	5.00	6
I	9	5.50	5
J	10	6.00	4
K	10½	6.50	3

Metric conversion chart

INCHES	MM	CM	INCHES	CM	INCHES	CM
⅛	3	0.3	9	22.9	30	76.2
¼	6	0.6	10	25.4	31	78.7
½	13	1.3	12	30.5	33	83.8
⅝	16	1.6	13	33.0	34	86.4
¾	19	1.9	14	35.6	35	88.9
⅞	22	2.2	15	38.1	36	91.4
1	25	2.5	16	40.6	37	94.0
1¼	32	3.2	17	43.2	38	96.5
1½	38	3.8	18	45.7	39	99.1
1¾	44	4.4	19	48.3	40	101.6
2	51	5.1	20	50.8	41	104.1
2½	64	6.4	21	53.3	42	106.7
3	76	7.6	22	55.9	43	109.2
3½	89	8.9	23	58.4	44	111.8
4	102	10.2	24	61.0	45	114.3
4½	114	11.4	25	63.5	46	116.8
5	127	12.7	26	66.0	47	119.4
6	152	15.2	27	68.6	48	121.9
7	178	17.8	28	71.1	49	124.5
8	203	20.3	29	73.7	50	127.0